The intercession

BENNIE MOSTERT

Discover your calling to intercede with God for others

carpe diem MEDIA

THE POWER OF INTERCESSION
produced by Carpe Diem Media

First edition, first print 2007
ISBN 978-1-920156-43-5

Typesetting • Justine Horn
Editor & Translator • San-Mari Mills
Cover design and illustrations • Magdie Claasens
Printed and bound by CTP Book Printers

CONTACT DETAILS
Carpe Diem Media
P O Box 5801 Vanderbijlpark 1900
Tel • (016) 982 3617 Fax • (016) 982 3618 E-mail • boeke@carpediem.co.za

Website
www.carpediem.co.za

CONTENTS

The power is not in intercession, the power is in God and in Him alone. Our focus must never be intercession. God is our focus, God our Father and his Son Jesus Christ through the power of the Holy Spirit.

PREFACE

"We are all dwarfs standing on the shoulders of giants", a wise man once said. I have read much during the years. Books by Andrew Murray, A.W. Tozer, Roy Hession, Henri Nouwen, J.I. Packer, Madame Guyon, Fenelon, Jessie Penn-Lewis, Oswald J. Smith, manuscripts of the Egyptian desert monks, theological books, dozens of books on prayer, biographies, etc. Where I have been able to acknowledge, I did so. Concepts and ideas of other writers are incorporated in places, but are often difficult to indicate. These are my insights into and understanding of this topic as it has taken shape in me through the years, in acknowledgement of the fact that I drank from many fountains. What you will read are not new laws and by no means the last and final word on the topic. Take what is a blessing to you and leave the rest.

Intercession is one of a Christian's most essential privileges and responsibilities. It is part of our priestly role. Intercession is not in opposition to worship, praise, thanksgiving, personal requests and other forms of prayer, and it does not replace these either. No form of prayer is more important or "more spiritual" than any other. This book explains intercession in more depth and wishes to emphasise the importance of intercession.

PROLOGUE

It was Rees Howells who said in a crisis situation during World War II: "Prayer has failed and only intercession will take us through." This might sound strange to many people; it did to me the first time I heard it. During the past many years I came to a better understanding of intercession. It has been a difficult but exciting road.

I am convinced that if the church in South Africa and worldwide is at all interested in making progress with the commission to make disciples of all nations, prayer alone will not be enough. We will have to turn to intercession. The aim of this book is to explain the difference between prayer and intercession and to clarify the different facets and effect of intercession.

As a church, we should take action and proceed to "attack", and launch an offensive against the wave of darkness that is flooding the world. Satan is not going to sit back and watch humankind being saved. He is going to fight. Let us not be daunted by this battle. It is astounding how the church has started praying for revival and for the evangelisation of unreached ethnic groups. It is as if the church has awakened from a long winter sleep and suddenly realised that the Great Commission in Matthew 28:19-20 has still not been accomplished after 2000 years. There is a very clear link between prayer and the accomplishment of the Great Commission. A major prayer movement in India talks of *The Greater Commission* when referring to Matthew 9:38: *"Ask* [pray] *the Lord of the harvest, therefore, to send out workers into his harvest field."* Their argument is that not all Christians are called by God to go out as "full-time" workers, but that *all* Christians are called upon to pray for the harvest and for the workers.

It is my desire that the church will not just *talk* about prayer, but that the church will *pray*. However, the church must pray for more than just the sick in hospitals, new church buildings, new carpets for the church, and a better sound system for the worship and praise team. When the main prayer focus of the church moves to the unsaved, the unreached, revival, the destruction of the strongholds of Evil and the advancement of the kingdom, and does not concentrate only on maintenance, a new day will dawn for the church. This day has already dawned in many countries and in many churches. The church *has* started praying again.

My prayer is that this book will give guidelines to those who are serious about prayer, to guide them towards a deeper understanding of the responsibility of the church towards prayer, as well as that of the individual, and for the privilege that we have to pray and thus be co-workers of God in the gathering of the harvest.

What is intercession?

The English word *intercession* is from the Latin verb *intercedo*, which means "to go between, to intervene, to protest, against, oppose, mediate". From the verb *intercedo* is the noun *intercessor,* which means "preventer" or "mediator"; literally the one who goes between.

The act of intercession occurs in many instances in daily life:

When an advocate handles legal actions; when an attorney draws up contracts for his clients and in this manner acts as mediator or a go-between; when parties in the corporate world make use of mediators to assist in resolving conflict; when a government sends an ambassador to a foreign country to represent his/her own country and to talk on behalf of this country. Intercession has the character of delegation and authority, delegated authority.

It boils down to the fact that an intercessor is a *representative.*

In a Biblical context the concept intercession comes to the fore in various ways: Intercession took place when Jesus died for us on the cross; God appointed Adam as his representative, delegate, yes as intercessor, on earth; intercession took place when Moses interceded with God for forty days and nights without food, and pleaded with God not to destroy his people for worshipping the golden calf; the Holy Spirit came to act as intercessor, to represent the Holy Trinity in us as believers, to remind us of Jesus' words and to help us when we pray.

It is particularly in the life of Jesus and in prayer that intercession is most clearly portrayed in the Bible.

Intercessory prayer

Prayer can take on many forms. There is praise, worship, confession of sins, thanksgiving, personal prayer requests, etc. And then there is intercessory prayer.

In 1 Timothy 2:1, we read about different forms of prayer: *requests, petitions, prayers, intercession* and *thanksgiving. Prayer* is clearly distinguished from *intercession.*

Thus intercessory prayer means that someone "goes or comes between, protests or opposes, mediates" and in this manner literally becomes an intercessor or mediator, literally the one who comes between. The Greek word *entunchano* is the same as the Latin word *intercedo.* The Greek word *entunchano* can be translated as "to plead for a person, to request." And this is precisely what intercession means.

Jeremiah and Moses demonstrate intercession

Jeremiah 18:20b is a "definition" of intercession: *Remember that*

I stood before you and spoke on their behalf to turn your wrath away from them. We find another example in Psalm 106:23: *So he* [God] *said he would destroy them – had not Moses, his chosen one, stood in the breach before him to keep his wrath from destroying them.* Intercession takes place where a person prays for a third party, someone else. The prayer does not focus on our own needs, but on the needs of others, a third party. This is exactly what Moses and Jeremiah did. They pleaded with God for Israel.

Intercession is *"Paga"*

The word intercession in the Old Testament is from the root *paga,* which means "meet, request, intervene or come between", where someone speaks to God on behalf of a third party. Thus intercession means to stand between God and a third party, someone else. Basically it never means to pray for your own needs. Worship, request, confession do not need more than two parties whereas intercession does.

The intercessor enters into *paga* with God, he meets with God. The intercessor is someone who enters into God's presence, meets with God and speaks to Him. He pleads with God, intervenes and asks God to act in a specific situation. Jesus entered into *paga* with God, He met with God, intervened for us, stood between God and us. The fact that Jesus "stood in the breach" between God and us, cost Him his life. In Isaiah 53:12 we read: *... he* [Jesus] *bore the sin of many, and made intercession (paga) for the transgressors.*

The intercessor meets with God and "arranges/organises" meetings between God and people. Yes, of course we cannot "organise" or "make arrangements" for God. It is simply a manner of speaking. The intercessor asks that God will meet with a person. When I intercede for someone, I request a meeting between God and the sick person, or a meeting between God and the unsaved person.

When intercessors pray, there is a meeting between God and the intercessor and as a result of this, a meeting is "set up" between God and a third person.

The word matchmaker refers to someone who arranges for two people, a man and a woman, to meet. A matchmaker brings the two people together. Intercessors are matchmakers – they arrange meetings between God and people, between the Bridegroom (Jesus) and the Bride (the church = people).

Intercession is a position before God

Intercession is a position before God, a spiritual position. We stand before God in a spiritual sense, on behalf of a third person or cause, and we pray to the Lord about it. This position is a 24-hour position. It is not a five-minutes-a-day occurrence. The intercessor stands in the breach before God and pleads *until* the Lord answers. He does not leave this position, he stays there 24 hours a day.

You might be quick to retort, "Surely I cannot pray 24 hours a day, seven days a week." Quite right. That is why it is a spiritual position. As intercessor I stand before God spiritually for a specific cause. At times I use words, at other times there are no words, merely a groaning. At times the intercessor prays for hours, at other times the intercessor just spends the day at the throne, and reminds God of the matter. But in the spiritual sphere the intercessor stands before God until the matter has been completed, until the answer has been given.

I have been praying for revival for more than 28 years. Many other believers I have come across have been praying for it much longer. Sometimes days and even weeks or longer pass where I do not pray for it specifically, but *spiritually* I remain standing before God for this cause. At times I leave my spiritual position, then God calls me back to come and stand in the breach. Over the past few years I have been standing before the Lord with new expectation, because I believe that God wants to give revival. Sometimes people ask me, "If God has not given revival after so many years of prayer, why do you keep on praying?" My answer is quite simple: "God would not encourage and call upon me to pray for revival these many years if He does not want to give revival."

Intercessors pray for grace and mercy rather than judgment

It is clear from Psalm 106:23 and Ezekiel 22:30-31 that intercessors are focused on God. They pray to God to ward off the judgment. They pray that God will be merciful and compassionate. Intercessors are not in the first place worried about Satan and his demonic forces. Satan is of secondary importance. Take a look at Ezekiel 22:30: *I looked up for a man among them who would build up the wall and stand before me in the gap on behalf of the land so that I would not have to destroy it ...*

The intercessor stands in the gap, but he/she is facing God – pleading for grace and mercy.

More than general prayer

Intercession is more than generalised prayer. There is intensity in intercession that is not found in ordinary prayer. It is not a personal prayer request. Intercession is not the same as supplication. It includes supplication, but it is more than supplication. Intercession is thanksgiving, worship, praise and confession of sin, but it is also more.

By means of intercession we have authority on earth, we rule on earth. Psalm 115:16 says that the Lord has given the earth to the people, this is where we should rule. Romans 5:17 calls upon us to *reign* on earth through Jesus Christ. Intercession is a position before the Lord, a spiritual position and a position of power. In Ezekiel 22:30 the Lord is looking for a man to stand before Him in the breach on behalf of the land so that He will not destroy the land. This indicates intercession, someone who takes a spiritual position before God and intervenes, comes between, pleads that God will not destroy the city and the land. If God does not find someone to do this, then his judgment will come over them (Ezek 22:31).

The fruits of intercession

Intercessory prayer has a powerful effect. It changes the future and destiny of individuals, churches, ethnic groups and nations.

1. Intercession influences the destiny of cities and nations

God has the destiny of nations and countries in his hands. In 1 Timothy 2:1-2 we learn that we need to pray for kings and all those in authority by means of intercession and thanksgiving.

In Daniel 2:20-21 we read: ***Praise be to the name of God forever and ever, wisdom and power are his. He changes times and seasons; he sets up kings and deposes them. He gives wisdom to the wise and knowledge to the discerning. "If at any time I announce that a nation or kingdom is to be uprooted, torn down and destroyed, and if that nation I warned repents of***

its evil, then I will relent and not inflict on it the disaster I had planned. And ... at another time I announce that a nation or kingdom is to be built up and planted ..."

Now read these two passages in conjunction with Ezekiel 22:30-31: *"I looked for a man among them who would build up the wall and stand before me in the gap on behalf of the land so that I would not have to destroy it, but I found none. So I will pour out my wrath on them and consume them with my fiery anger, bringing down on their own heads all they have done ..."*

What do these passages tell us? God rules the world. He is in control of nations and countries. If countries and nations sin, God punishes them, but if they repent, God announces his mercy on them. In Ezekiel 22:30-31 God makes a direct connection between his mercy and judgment, and intercession. When nations sin, God wants the intercessor to act as a go-between, to plead that God will have mercy. This is what Ezekiel 22:30-31 teaches us.

Long before Ezekiel, God called Elijah to pray for Israel. Israel had started serving Baal and other idols. This enraged God. God looked for someone to stand in the breach for Israel. He found Elijah. Elijah prayed (1 Kings 17-18) – God heard him and the people turned back to God.

In Genesis 18 God came to Abraham and told him that He wanted to destroy Sodom and Gomorrah. Abraham did exactly what God wanted Him to do – he started pleading for Sodom and Gomorrah to be saved. At first it seemed as if Abraham did not succeed, but God heard his prayer.

There is more than enough evidence that God changes the future of nations and countries through the prayers of his children.

2. Intercession leads to the conversion of people

The church in Acts was a church that prayed. We read in Acts 1 how they were joined together constantly in prayer until the Holy Spirit was poured out. Time and time again after this we read how they met daily in different homes to pray together (Acts 2:42-47).We read how they prayed for Peter when he was in prison and the miracle that was performed in answer to these prayers (Acts 12). We read how the apostles met and prayed amid persecution. In answer to their prayers God shook the place where they met, and signs and wonders took place (Acts 4:23 etc).

However, the prayers of the first church led mainly to the salvation of people. Acts tells it like this:

- On the day of the Pentecost *3 000* people repented and became converted.
- Acts 2:47 says that *every day* the Lord added people who were saved to the church.
- In Acts 4:4, a few weeks after the pouring out of the Holy Spirit, the number of believers had already grown to *5 000.*
- Acts 5:14 tells us how *more and more men and women were added* to the number of believers.
- Acts 6:7 speaks of *a large number of priests* who became believers and that the number of believers in Jerusalem *increased rapidly.*
- Acts 8:14 writes about the people of *Samaria* who started accepting the word of God.
- Acts 13:48 tells us that, in reaction to Paul and Barnabas' preaching, *all who were appointed for eternal life believed.*

What reasons can be given for the rapid spreading of the gospel during the first century? One of them is most certainly the fact that believers prayed. The church prayed, and God answered.

During the past few decades, the church of Christ, worldwide, has started praying again. What is the result of this tremendous prayer revival? One very obvious and distinct result is the number of people who are currently being added to the church:

- In 1987 it was calculated that at least 70 000 people were being added to the church of Christ daily. At the beginning of 1998, approximately 180 000 people were being added to the church of Christ daily.
- Bible believing Christians were at that stage growing at a rate of 6, 9% per annum, more than twice as fast as Islam and three time faster than the growth of the world population.
- In Africa, south of the Sahara, the church was growing daily by 24 000 to 28 000 people. In China the church was growing by 30 000 to 35 000 people per day. Towards the end of the past century in China alone, an estimated 25 million people became converted to Christianity over a period of four years.
- At the beginning of this century, with the great worldwide revival from 1900 to 1910, an estimated five million members had joined the church worldwide. Presently, five million members are joining the church every thirty days.

There is power in prayer. Intercession leads to the salvation of people. The figures given above are an indication of the effect of prayer in the lives of the unsaved.

3. Intercession leads to the destruction of the works of the Evil One

It is important to understand that in essence, intercession is also a declaration of war against the forces of Evil. It is a powerful instrument in the Lord's hand to break the strongholds and power of the Evil One and resist Satan's attacks. Intercession in the form of warfare prayer has a powerful influence in the spiritual sphere.

4. Intercession sets the angels of God in motion, with the accompaniment of signs, wonders, powerful deeds and the gifts of the Holy Spirit

Intercession sets the angels of God in motion. We do however need to say, radically and clearly: we must never pray to angels and try to give them direct instructions. God rules over the angels. God tells the angels to act, how and when.

Currently there is a marked increase in the activity of angels. In Hebrews 1:14 we read that angels are ministering spirits in God's service and that they are sent out by Him to serve those who will inherit salvation.

In Turkey with its 65 million inhabitants there were an estimated 3 000 Christians at the beginning of 1998. Especially in the preceding five years an increasing number of Turks became converted. It is interesting that according to the missionaries working in the country, approximately 35% of all Turks became converted as a result of the appearance of angels, or dreams and visions people had.

We read in Hebrews 2:4: *God also testifies to it by signs, wonders and various miracles, and gifts of the Holy Spirit distributed according to his will.* God is a "co-worker" by means of signs, wonders, the ministry of angels, powerful deeds and the gifts of the Holy Spirit.

Daniel prayed and God answered by sending an angel to bring him a message. This angel was also involved in an intense spiritual battle with the demonic prince of Greece and Persia (Dan 10:13, 20). In 2 Kings 6:17-20, Elisha prayed to God and asked the Lord to open the eyes of his slave so that he could see the army of angels around the city: *Then the Lord opened the servant's eyes, and he looked and saw the hills full of horses and chariots of fire all around Elisha.*

Especially from Moslem countries there have recently been astonishing stories of the activities of angels, signs, wonders and powerful deeds. In Northern Iraq a Moslem man walked up a hill one evening. Suddenly he saw a brightly lit cross in front of him and someone who said to him that Jesus is the Way, the Truth and the Life. In another country in the Middle East a fanatical fundamentalist Moslem leader swore an oath that he would annihilate all Christians. One night Jesus stood by his side in a dream and said to him, "Stop persecuting my church, build it." He also became converted and the following day told 150 Moslems what had happened to him. All 150 were converted. In Bulgaria 24 Moslem *imams* (spiritual leaders) came together for a meeting in May 1993. According to them Jesus appeared in their midst and talked to them. They became converted and today all 24 mosques are Christian churches. During 1990 in Algiers the Lord appeared to at least one individual in each of approximately 400 houses by means of an extraordinary miracle. Practically every person in that specific village began to follow Jesus. Soon more than 50 000 Moslems in that area had become converted.

5. Intercession prepares the way for revival and the powerful working of the Holy Spirit.

The history of the past 300 years is full of stories of intercessors who grabbed hold of God in desperate prayer, and in answer to their prayers saw communities receive the Holy Spirit and God favouring them with revival.

In Acts 1-2 we read how the prayers of the Christians led to the outpouring of the Holy Spirit.

In 1857 Jeremiah Lanphier sent invitations to people to meet in the Fulton Street church in New York for prayer. They would pray that God would deliver the country from the most devastating economic and spiritual crisis. The first Wednesday 6 people turned up. The second week there were 20, then 40 and in a month's time 100 people came to pray on a Wednesday afternoon between 12:00-13:00. Within six months there were tens of thousands of people in New York who came together in different halls and churches to seek God in prayer. Someone who travelled to New York told people how he saw during his journey of almost 2 000 kilometres, Christians praying in every place. In the mornings before work, during lunchtimes and in the evenings people came together to pray. Within two years 2 million new converts joined churches. This did not include the great numbers of "dead" members within the church who experienced revival. This revival spread to Wales, Northern Ireland and various other countries. In 1860 revivals started in the Southern and Western Cape and thousands became converted; entire communities experienced revival. As in the USA, the revival in South Africa was a prayer revival. God gave revival in answer to prayer.

The abovementioned is but one example. There are many more, like the revival on the Hebrides Islands to the Northwest of Scotland and the revival in Wales during the second half of 1904. Revival and prayer are inseparable; part and parcel of each other.

The focus of intercession

What does God want from us?

What does God have in mind? What should we pray for at this stage? What are the prayer burdens of the Holy Spirit? These are questions the church should be asking at present. It is necessary now, more than ever before, that we as prophetic intercessors should do and pray what God has in mind for us.

I believe there are seven areas or matters that are near to God's heart at present. They are of course not the only areas, but I am convinced that the church of Jesus Christ should intercede intensively for these matters.

a. World evangelism

The commission in Matthew 28:19-20 has not yet been accomplished: *"Go and make disciples of all nations."* It is a very clear command. The word "nations" used here is the Greek word *ethnoi* that literally means "all ethnic groups". God's command is that all ethnic groups must be made disciples.

In Matthew 24:3-51 Jesus foretells the future. The passage starts with a question that the disciples asked the Lord Jesus: *"Tell us", they said, "when will this happen, and what will be the sign of your coming and of the end of the age?"* Take note that the disciples do not ask for "signs", but for one "sign". Jesus explains a good many things and gives them many signs that they must be on the lookout for, but in verse 14 He gives them one sign that will be the indication that the end is near: *"And this gospel of the kingdom will be preached in the whole world as a testimony to all nations, and then the end will come."* The one sign therefore, is when all the nations (*ethnoi* = ethnic groups) have heard the gospel.

The gospel must be preached to all the unreached, to the lost, those who have never heard it before. At the beginning of 1998 there were still one billion, that is to say 1000 million people who had not ever, not even once, heard the gospel. Of the 5,8 billion people on earth, only 1,9 billion were nominal Christians. The number of evangelical Christians or Christian believers in the Scriptures, were approximately 800 million, more or less 14% of the world population. There is much work to be done.

The task of the church is not only maintenance. The kingdom of God must grow. All the nations must hear the gospel. There is a lot of *prayer work* ahead.

- We must pray for open doors. Especially in the Moslem countries, among the Hindus and Buddhists it is important. But also in the secularised Western world new open doors are necessary so that the gospel can be taken to people.
- We must pray for the breaking down of the strongholds of Evil. Millions of people are caught up in the occult, demonic religions and many are being misled.
- We must pray for finances. One of the greatest obstacles in

proclaiming the gospel is funds.

- We must pray for more workers.
- Missionary work and evangelisation are the responsibility of the church. We must pray that the church, in particular congregations themselves, take responsibility for the commission to reach the nations. The church has been given the mandate and only the church can reach the unreached and unsaved with the gospel.

b. Unity in the body of Christ

Many books have been written on unity in the church and hundreds of meetings are held annually on church unity. But how seldom people pray for unity in the church.

Jesus prays in John 17 that we will be one. Jesus is coming back to fetch his bride, the church. He is not coming back to fetch a divided, depressed and devastated church. He is coming back to a church that is prepared to meet the Master. We are told in Revelation 19:7 of the wedding of the Lamb and of the bride: *"... and his bride has made herself ready."*

A divided church has an enfeebled testimony for the world. Jesus paid the price in full so that we can stand before Him as his bride without stain or blemish and so that we can be one like the Father and the Son are one.

Unity and cooperation within the body of Christ are imperative if we are going to impact the world and if we want to succeed in bringing the gospel to the unreached. No single church or denomination can carry out the commission by itself. We need the whole body to complete the task of world evangelisation. We have all the expertise, all the money, all the technical skills, all the people that are necessary to complete the work. The one thing that we're short of is unity.

Many people are afraid of unity. Of course there is false unity that wishes to promote the implementation of a single world rule. "New Age" unity and other false forms of solidarity. Our unity however, is in Jesus Christ, in obeying Him, his Word, the Holy Spirit and God's instructions. Not all unity is wrong. We need to be watchful and alert, but we must not allow the Evil One to estrange us from our brothers and sisters who have been washed in blood and are included in God's Kingdom.

We must pray for this unity. We must pray that Christians will work together and live together in new and stronger covenant relationships. This unity is not optional. In this respect Ecclesiastes 4:12 comes to mind: *Though one may be overpowered, two can defend themselves. A cord of three strands is not quickly broken.*

c. The restoration of Israel

Pray for the restoration of Israel. Israel played a key role through the entire history of humankind. It will be the case up until the end. God still has a specific purpose and plan with Israel.

Take careful note of the following words in Acts 3:2: *"... heaven must receive the Lord Jesus until the times of restoration of all things which God has spoken by the mouth of all his Holy prophets since the world began."* We are now living in a time of restoration where everything prophesied by the prophets of long ago will come to fulfilment. Take Daniel in Daniel 9. He was busy reading Jeremiah's prophecy when he discovered that the time had now come and that Israel had to return to their country after 70 years of exile. On the grounds of the prophetic word in Jeremiah, Daniel started praying (Dan 9:4-19). In Micah 5 we read that the prophet announced in advance that the Messiah would be born in Bethlehem. 500 years later the Christ is born just there. In Isaiah 53 the suffering of the Messiah is announced in advance in great detail. Hundreds of years later it happened exactly like this.

God's prophetic word must be brought to fulfilment. But it will be accompanied by restoration, and part of that restoration, as is prophesied, is the restoration of Israel. The prophetic books of the Old Testament bear ample testimony to that. It was prophesied in advance that the Jews would return to their country. It was brought to fulfilment in 1948, exactly as prophesied. God's prophetic word stands firm. In Romans 9-11 Paul explains that a period will come in which Israel will be restored and in great numbers they will be converted to Christianity (Rom 11:12).

The church must pray for the salvation of the Jews and the restoration of Israel.

d. Workers

Matthew 9:38 teaches us to pray to the Lord of the harvest to send out workers into his harvest field. The Greek word here translated as "pray" or "ask", is the word *deomai* which means "to plead, call, beg/supplication". The root of the word is *deo*, which means "bind". The word *deomai* is a strong word and in the context that it is used, it has the meaning of intercession. This asks the intercessor to approach God with intense intercession and to plead with Him to send workers into the harvest field.

We read in Matthew 9:36: *When he* [Jesus] *saw the crowds, he had compassion on them, because they were harassed and helpless, like sheep without a shepherd.* Jesus was compassionate and that is why He went to the people and proclaimed the kingdom of God to them. The command of God the Father is clear, but many Christians do not have compassion. And that is why they do not take the gospel to the unsaved and the unreached. We should pray for compassion in the hearts of people so that they will get up and go and obey God's command.

In Matthew 9:38 we are told to pray that God will "send out" workers into the harvest field. The Greek word used here is *ekballo.* It is also the word that is used when the Bible says that Jesus drove out demons. The word literally means to drive out, to force out, to press or put pressure on. It is also used to describe the process in which the grapes are put through a wine press to force the juice from them. Thus Jesus is literally saying that we should plead with the Lord to whom the harvest belongs, to force workers into the harvest fields.

A calculation made by the *AD 2000 and Beyond Movement,* makes it clear that if we want to give the gospel *to* this generation *in* this generation, we need at least 200 000 new workers. So, let us pray for workers.

e. Spiritual leaders

Leaders in the church are under immense pressure. There are different reasons for this. There is a definite movement of the Holy Spirit and we literally see millions of new converts every year. David Barrette indicates that the church of Christ shows a nominal growth of 67 million people annually. A good 40-50% of these are converts. In China, over a period of four years, approximately 25 million people became converted to Christianity. There are not enough leaders to make disciples of these converts. The same is true of Africa and many Moslem countries where an increasing number of people are becoming converted.

Satan hates what is busy happening and one of his direct targets is church leaders. Every year there are many church leaders who leave the ministry because they have lost hope amidst the constant strife and struggle. Others are attacked by illness and yet others experience demonic attacks. Others commit sin in various ways and have to leave the ministry.

It is however, also encouraging to see that we are currently living in a time of restoration. During the course of the past few years the Lord has restored a considerable number of church leaders and they are once again busy serving the Lord, fully committed. Let us keep on praying for the restoration of leaders who have fallen, have lagged behind or become discouraged.

Church members should build a wall of prayer around their ministers and pastors. In my own life I experience every day, the influence and strength of a group of personal intercessors who pray for me, my family and my ministry daily. Without them I cannot do the work I currently do. If there is one thing I would like to recommend to ministers and pastors, it would be to put in place a team of personal intercessors to pray for them. I would strongly recommend the book *Prayer Partners* by John Maxwell.

This matter cannot be emphasised strongly enough. Church members should hold up the hands of their ministers and pastors as Aaron and Hur held up Moses' hands. The battle is too fierce, the burden too heavy that preachers must bear. So let us pray for them.

f. Revival

During September 1997 I had the privilege of meeting an elderly man of God. His name is Wesley Duewel and he is a man familiar with intercession. We had spoken for a few minute only when he remarked, "The Holy Spirit does not make fools of us. All over the world the Holy Spirit is calling on people to start praying. If God were not serious about revival, He would not summon us to pray."

God urges hundreds of thousands, yes, millions of believers, all over the world to pray for revival. God is serious about spiritual revival. Without spiritual revival the church would not have the strength and vitality to fulfil the Great Commission. The gospel must be taken to all nations and it is the task of the church to do so. Revival is not an option, it is a spiritual must.

In many places people are praying for revival. There is a growing and living expectancy that we will see revival soon. "The Lord very clearly told us that the revival would start here in the Cape," someone said to me on occasion when I was in the Cape. A few weeks later in East London someone came up to me and said exactly the same thing: they were convinced that the Lord told them the revival would start in East London. Months later, I heard the same in Durban, Bloemfontein and in almost every place I visited.

And I am convinced that this is the way it will be. I realise there are people who will immediately respond in a way that seems to be more logical: "But surely that is impossible! It could only start in one town and then spread to other towns and cities." That's what I also thought until I had a dream one night. The Lord had never before spoken to me in dreams, although I know that God uses dreams.

In my dream I was walking somewhere in Pretoria. It was in one of Pretoria's lovely parks and I was walking past a few trees when I came across some wild lilies. I stopped and, amazed, I looked at these lilies. They were all in bud and would open in a day or two. While I stood watching, one of the flowers opened. I called out, "Look, here the lily is opening in front of my eyes." And as I was saying it, all the lilies opened at the same time. The next morning when I woke up, I thought about this dream and told myself this would most probably be the way revival will come. It will come in different places, as people experienced the Lord telling them this, but it will happen all at once. It will not be necessary to fetch the "fire" elsewhere.

God gives revival. General and countrywide revival is a mighty and sovereign act performed by God. Our task as humans is to prepare the road to revival with prayer. We cannot fabricate or produce revival. We can only prepare the way by means of persistent, intense prayer.

g. The poor and the needy

Jesus says in Luke 4:18-19: *"The Spirit of the Lord is on me, because he has anointed me to preach good news for the poor … to proclaim freedom for the prisoners and recovery of sight for the blind, to release the oppressed, to proclaim the year of the Lord's favor."* God prioritises the poor and the needy. Isaiah 58 is about fasting, but it also explains God's heart for the poor, the oppressed and the needy.

Unfortunately the so-called evangelical Christians in the past did not pay enough attention to the mandate that the Bible gives Christians to bring the gospel in all its facets, thus also to the poor and needy. Too often the focus was on the spiritual need of people and not also on the physical. The Scriptures pay an exceptional amount of attention to the physical needs of people. Read the Bible with an honest, open mind and discover what the Lord says about the poor, needy and oppressed.

Almost 30% of the world's population can be classified as poor and needy. This group of people is not a fringe phenomenon in society. Three out of every ten people fall in this category. These are people in need and God gives us the Holy Spirit to reach them with the gospel and its full consequences (spiritual and social).

The Christian has been commissioned to see to the need of the poor. We should pray for the need of the poor in deadly earnest and intensity. Each church should make it a part of their prayer calendar.

4

The power of united intercession

Deuteronomy 32:30: 1+1 = 10 000

There are many interesting examples in nature that we could use to explain teamwork. Did you know that a weight of up to 4 ton can be drawn by one horse? And did you know that a weight of 22 ton can be drawn by 2 horses? Thus, when there are two horses their potential is not doubled, it increases *fivefold.*

We also see this principle very clearly in the Scriptures. Let us first take a look at Joshua 23:10: *One of you routs a thousand, because the Lord your God fights for you, just as he promised.* One person is able to complete an immense job in the kingdom of God: he can chase "a thousand". See also Psalm 3:7: *I will not fear the tens of thousands drawn up against me on every side.* This means that the "strong" among us could fearlessly face even "ten thousand" or make them turn on their heel, but what happens if the onslaught is more than a "thousand" or "ten thousand"?

The Bible has an answer for this: The first is Leviticus 26:8: *Five of you will chase a hundred, and a hundred of you will chase ten thousand, and your enemies will fall by the sword before you.* Take careful note of the principle: five chase one hundred and a hundred chase ten thousand. Mathematically calculated, a hundred are supposed to chase two thousand. Yet, it happens in the spiritual sphere that when believers join hands, their strength is multiplied by five according to Leviticus 26:8. The other verse is Deuteronomy 32:30: *How could one man chase a thousand, or two put ten thousand to flight, unless their Rock has sold them, unless the Lord had given them up?* God finds it honourable when believers work together and when there is unity among his children. In this quotation, two should in fact defeat two thousand, but because God honours their unity and the fact that they work together, their strength multiplies exponentially.

An important spiritual secret is contained in these two passages from Scripture. It is also the key to victory over the strongholds of Evil. It has the potential that we need as believers to win the world for Christ. These two passages are confirmed by the pronouncement of Jesus Christ in Matthew 18:19-20: *"Again, I tell you that if two of you on earth agree about anything you ask for, it will be done for you by my Father in heaven. For where two or three come together in my name, there I am with them."* Note the reference to two or three. The word "agree" means to be in harmony with each other and this is indicative of unity. It is clear that the Lord Jesus says that spiritually something different and something more happens when two or three believers agree, join hands and take on a task together, yes, stand together in his Name. This passage has a very clear message for all who pray. The obvious meaning is that there is greater strength and greater certainty of an answer to prayer where two or three pray together.

There is more: In Ecclesiastes 4:12 we read: *Though one may be overpowered, two can defend themselves. A cord of three strands is not easily broken.* Churches, Christian organisations and prayer groups who work together, will see more significant breakthroughs in the kingdom of God. It is also quite clear that the spiritual and demonic onslaughts on the church of Christ are rapidly increasing. If we want to withstand this and gain the victory, we will have to stand together, united. In Exodus 17, Moses, Aaron and Hur pray on the mountain as a team, in a united, joint effort, while Joshua is fighting the Amalekites down below. Through Moses' intercession, with the help of Aaron and Hur, Joshua gains the victory over the Amalekites.

Paul writes in 2 Corinthians 1:11: *... as you help us by our prayers. Then many will give thanks on our behalf for the gracious favour granted us in answer to the prayers of many.* Note the word "many". It is not there by chance. There is strength in the combined prayer of "many" who pray. We often look at Elijah as a man who prayed powerfully, and indeed he did. But it is also important to take note of 1 Kings 19:18: *Yet I reserve seven thousand in Israel – all whose knees have not bowed down to Baal and all whose mouths have not kissed him.* There were seven thousand who, like Elijah, did not bend the knee to Baal. Elijah's prayer was important, but the seven thousand also prayed and God also heard their prayers; thus they contributed towards the revival that followed Elijah's prayers and God's intervention in 1 Kings 18. Paul calls upon all believers, all the believers in Rome and all the believers in Ephesus to join him by praying with him in his struggle (Rom 15:30-31; Eph 6:18).The prayer of one believer is powerful, but there is something exceptional about the prayers of two or more.

Focused and concentrated prayer

One of the principles of successful warfare is known as the *concentration of forces.* The general analyses the battlefield and determines which important strategic points should be attacked and taken into possession. More troops, canons, etc. are then concentrated on those points.

Our prayers should be focused and concentrated prayers. When we pray we should, as it were, "carry together, as one". In Matthew 18:19-20 there is a promise that says when two or three of us agree with each other in prayer, we will get from God what we ask for. The Greek word for agree is *sumphoneo,* and its literal meaning is to be in harmony, or in this sense then it could also be translated as "unanimity", which in turn can be described as "shared by everyone in a group" or "complete agreement about something among a group of people". The word agree would have no meaning if it were not applied to at least two people. Jesus calls upon believers, Christians, the church to agree with one another, to be in harmony with one another when they pray. When we are in harmony with one another, agree with one another, we will be able to pray as one. Then we will be able to carry as one the prayer burdens that God gives us.

We, as believers, should start to focus our prayers on strategic points. The victories that are gained in this way are of the utmost importance for the advancement of the kingdom. It is clear that the Lord calls the church to be in agreement, to join hands as they focus on certain prayer targets. Why? Because prayer is more powerful where people are joined together in prayer; there is more power in the prayers of many (2 Cor 1:8-11). For worldwide revival the prayers of one or two believers will not be enough. It will take the church of the Lord, joined together in prayer, united intercession of the church of the Lord, worldwide. To break through the strongholds of Islam, Buddhism, Hinduism and the New Age Movement will need a bigger prayer effort than the prayers of one or two congregations, churches or organisations.

The fruits that resulted the past few years from the *Pray Through the Window* as well as the *30 Days Moslem Prayer Focus,* and these are but two international initiatives, were exceptional. The reaction to the prayers of millions that participated in these prayer efforts confirms the power, urgency and need for united, concentrated prayer.

Satan hates unity among believers, because he knows how much power is unleashed in the spiritual realm when believers pray together as one. That is why it happens time and again that as soon as a community starts with the work of God, the devil starts sowing dividedness. Here the following saying is very true: "Divide and rule." As long as the Evil One succeeds in dividing us, and each of us is busy with his or her own thing, he makes us weak.

Households must learn to unite in prayer before God and to pray together for matters that are in the interest of the family. Different denominations should unite and pray for matters concerning the country. And the believers from different countries should unite in prayer for matters which concern the world and the nations of the world.

There is great potential and power in praying together and the church must make use of this power. Could this be one of the "greater things" that Jesus talks about in John 14:12-14 – the fact that believers should stand united, pray together and work together, and in answer to that greater things can be done? John 14:12-14 should, among other things, be read in the context of a prayer and part of the interpretation of this verse should be sought in the concepts "prayer" and "unity". Jesus places a high premium on unity among believers. It is by our unity that the world can tell we are children of God.

It is in the light of this that national prayer networks are so utterly important. This aims to join believers together across the boundaries of language, countries and denominational barriers, to focus on specific prayer targets and strongholds of the Evil One. One such target is the united focus of Christians all over the world on Moslem countries. More than one billion people belong to Islam. A while back I was in contact with a group who was busy with a ten-year prayer plan for the Moslem world. At the same time another group was calling on millions of believers all over the world to intercede for the Moslem world with 30 days of fasting and praying. The two groups were not aware of each other. Our lack of cooperation is partly to blame for our insufficient progress in spreading the gospel to all nations, all over the world. The children of the Lord should talk to one another and share with each other the things the Spirit brings to their attention. The result should be that when the Holy Spirit talks to different people about the same matter, they should join in prayer and focus on those matters.

Intercession is a ministry of the body of Christ

In intercession there is room for the individual intercessor. But in essence, intercession is the ministry of the body of Christ. We read in 1 Corinthians 12:13 that we are all baptised by one Spirit into one body. The church of Christ is one body and we should function as a body. We are saturated with the Spirit. In Matthew 16:18 we read that the gates of hell will not overcome the *church, not* the *individual.* In Matthew 18 there is talk of the church (*ecclesia)* for the first time, which means that it is Jesus' promise that if we are in agreement in prayer, God will be in our midst and we will get what we ask for (Matt 18:19-20). This promise is in the direct context of the *church*, the body of Christ.

When we read the books Ephesians and Colossians, it is very

clear that the promises in those books refer to the *church*, the body of Christ, and not in the fist place to individuals. There is much emphasis on the body and on unity in the Bible. If that body does not move in unity, the Evil One could gain control and the power, image and glory of the Father are not seen. In John 17:22 we read that there is a direct connection between the glory of God and unity amongst believers. Where there is a lack of unity, there is a lack of the glory of God. Psalm 133:3 teaches us that where brothers live together, there the Lord bestows his blessing. Where there is unity and united prayer, the glory of God will come upon the believers and God's work will be exceptionally powerful.

A study of prayer in the book of Acts shows that there are more references to group prayer and prayer meetings than to the prayers of individuals. The 120 disciples came together for a prayer meeting in the upstairs room (Acts 1:14). The believers went from house to house, breaking bread and joining together in prayer (Acts 4:42, 46 and 5:42). In times of emergency and persecution they came together and joined in constant prayer (Acts 4:24 and Acts 12:12). The leaders in Antioch came together to fast and pray and then set apart Paul and Silas to go and do missionary work (Acts 13:1-3). Paul and Silas prayed while they were in prison (Acts 16:25). There are several more examples. The point I wish to make is this: The early church knew the power and importance of praying together – and they saw the fruits of this.

Praying together, united prayer, was part of the secret of the rapid progress of the gospel during the course of the first century.

5

A house of prayer for the nations

The Bible calls upon us to pray for the nations. God's Word says quite clearly in Matthew 21:13: ***"My house will be called a house of prayer ..."*** We read in Mark 11:17: ***"My house will be called a house of prayer for all nations."*** In Isaiah 56:7b it is written: ***"... for my house will be called a house of prayer for all nations."***

The prophet Isaiah made it very clear and Jesus confirmed it:

- The church must be a house of prayer.
- In this house of prayer believers must pray for all the nations.

This is an assignment God gives us, a clear and direct commission! It is however, true that most churches are not houses of prayer. There are individuals who pray, but Jesus confirmed that the church, and in practice every congregation, must be a house of prayer for the nations. A congregation cannot say, "This is not our vision." It's not a matter of vision, but a direct command and we can either obey or disobey it.

The commission is not to pray only for my own people or nation. The Bible makes it quite clear to pray for "the (all) people" and "(all) nations". Too many Christians have narrowed this commission down so that they pray only for their own people. It is true of Americans, Zulus, Germans, the English, Russians, etcetera.

Individuals as houses of prayer

In Corinthians 6:19-20 it is very clearly stated that every believer is a temple in whom the Holy Spirit lives. The word temple could also be translated as "house of God". Every believer is a house of God, and if every individual is a house of God, I must also be a house of prayer for the nations.

Thus the commission to be a house of prayer for the nations is not given only to the church, but also to every individual.

John Knox, the well-known sixteenth century Scottish preacher, called upon God for the salvation of the Scottish people: "Lord, give me Scotland or I die." God gave Knox Scotland. When he died the great majority of the Scottish population were devoted Christians. John Knox was a house of prayer for the Scots.

Adoniram Judson, the first American missionary to Burma, had seven prayer times a day: 03:00, 06:00, 09:00, 12:00, 18:00, 21:00 and 00:00. A few decades after his death 20% of the Burmese were Christians. Adoniram Judson was a house of prayer for the Burmese people.

Robert Moffat prayed constantly for seven years until God gave revival in what was then Bechuanaland (Botswana). Moffat was a house of prayer for the Bechuanas.

Nations as inheritance!

Romans 8:16-17 teaches us that we as children of God are also heirs of God, co-heirs with Christ. In Ephesians 1:3 Paul tells us that God blessed us in the heavenly realms with every spiritual blessing in Christ Jesus. 2 Corinthians 1:20 explains that all promises are "yes" in Christ Jesus and that we should say "Amen" to it, to the glory of God.

Now take all three these scriptures together: we are co-heirs with Christ, God blessed us in the heavenly realms with every spiritual blessing, and all promises are "yes" in Christ and, strictly speaking, we should make it a reality by saying "Amen" to it.

Psalm 2 is a prophetic psalm pointing to Jesus. In Psalm 2:8 God the Father promises Jesus nations, should He ask for these: *"Ask of me, and I will make the nations your inheritance, the ends of the earth your possession."* This is an exceptionally great and precious promise. The Hebrew word *sha'al*, which is used in Psalm 2:8, is a stronger word than "ask". It can also mean to demand. When God then says to us, "Ask me," He is in fact also saying, "Demand of me."

Take note: This promise was given to Jesus Christ. We are co-heirs with Christ. The content of this promise is for us too because we inherit together with Christ, according to Romans 8:17. Biblically we have the right to link Psalm 2:8 and Romans 8:17 and this gives us, before the throne of God, the lawful right to ask the Father to give us the nations, to make them our possession – this is part of our inheritance in Christ Jesus. When we pray for this in Jesus' Name, we will receive it from the Father. In the light of Romans 8:17 it makes sense that we, on the grounds of the fact that we are co-heirs with Christ, *demand our inheritance.*

Responsible heirs

What a privilege to be heirs, but as heirs we remain God's representatives on earth. Representation is accompanied by responsibilities and obligations. We have been given the commission, on the grounds of the work of Christ, to take the gospel to people. There is a task for us to complete.

Colossians 1:24-25: *Now I rejoice in what was suffered for you, and I fill up in my flesh what is still lacking in regard to Christ's afflictions, for the sake of his body, which is the church. I have become its servant by the commission God gave me to present to you the word of God in its fullness.*

Christ brought the perfect sacrifice. He paid the full price for the sins of the human race. We were appointed as God's representative on earth. It is our responsibility to go out and share with others Christ's perfected work on the cross. With his work on earth, his death on the cross and resurrection, He gave back to humankind our mandate as God's representatives on earth, which was partially lost because of the Fall. Humankind is still commissioned to be God's representatives. Humankind is still commissioned to build God's kingdom, to rule, govern, to care for his creation. In this process we are co-workers of Christ Jesus and the Holy Spirit. This was God's plan.

In Colossians 1:24-25 Paul says that he is busy fulfilling the Word of God by means of his suffering and labour. This work comprises the spreading of the gospel to all nations, the unreached, the unsaved.

Part of what needs to be fulfilled, is the following:

- The gospel must be brought to all people. We need to take the message of Christ's perfect sacrifice for our sins to the nations – this is the mission we need to accomplish (Matt 28:19-20).
- By means of our intercession (*paga)* we must impress upon God Christ's act of intercession and "arrange" meetings

between God and people. God calls upon us humans to act as intercessors so that Christ's act of intercession impacts people's lives. We must pray that He will save people and set them free of their sin.

- As Christ suffered for the sins of the world, so we must share in that suffering by proclaiming the gospel to humankind. Christ suffered for our sins, but we are co-heirs of the suffering of Christ (Rom 8:17; Col 1:24; Phil 3:10).
- We must carry the burdens of others away. In the same way that Christ carried our sins away on the cross, as scapegoat (Lev 16), the Word commissions us in Galatians 6:2 and Romans 15:1-3 to literally *carry away* the burdens of others. The Greek word *bastazo,* that is used here to describe that we should carry each other's burdens, literally means to "carry them away".
- We must support others and carry them so that they can remain standing. The Greek word *anechomai* that is used in Ephesians 4:2 and Colossians 3:13 to encourage us to bear with one another and to be patient with each other literally means "to support, to carry, to keep upright". Jesus carries us day by day, but God also gives us the instruction to carry others, to keep them on their feet, to support them.

In this way we complete what Christ started: He brought the perfect sacrifice. We must offer this perfect sacrifice to others. Jesus is the balm of Gilead, we must apply the balm. He is the fountain of life, we must take the living water to the people. God enabled us to "competently administer the new covenant" (2 Cor 3:6). We must hand out to others the salvation in Christ Jesus – God enabled us to do it. This is our mandate, it is our responsibility.

One of the most important ways in which we can minister the new covenant to others is by means of intercession. Our task as representatives of God is to bring people to God through intercession. In this way we complete what Christ started.

God rules through the prayers of his children

God rules through people and their prayers

Throughout the entire Bible it is clear that God chose to "limit" Himself by the decision to work through people where matters of the earth are concerned. Is this then not the reason why the earth is in such a state? Not because it is God's will, but because the people whom God gave the commission, the mandate to rule, do not take their responsibility seriously enough?

The Bible is clear on the matter that God rules over the earth together with, or through people. God is always looking for reliable men and women that He can entrust his work to. God is always looking for someone to work through.

God can fill the whole world with his glory and spread the Word of God rapidly all over the world, but He chooses to rule through our prayers when 2 Thessalonians 3:1 gives the command: *"... pray ... that the message of the Lord may spread rapidly and be honored, just as it was with you ..."*

God used the prayers of Elijah and Job

In 1 Kings 18 we read how God used the Prayers of Elijah to bring his will to fruition. In 1 Kings 18 we read that God tells Elijah: *"Go and present yourself to Ahab, and I will send rain on the land."* God wants to give rain, but God decides in accordance with his agreement with humankind as his representative on earth, that Elijah should pray for rain. God used Elijah's prayers to bring rain again. In I Kings 18:41-45 we read that Elijah climbed to the top of the mountain Carmel and prayed. He prayed seven times. Why did he pray seven times? Seven is, among other things, the number for completion in the Scriptures. To bring the matter to completion, conclude it, bring it to an end, Elijah had to pray seven times. Only then the rain came. God could have given the rain without Elijah's prayers, but He did not. Elijah's prayers were necessary; God "used" them to bring rain.

We read in Job 42:7-8: ... [the Lord] *said to Eliphaz the Temanite, "I am angry with you and your two friends ... take seven bulls and seven rams and go to my servant Job and sacrifice a burnt offering for yourselves. My servant Job will pray for you, and I will accept his prayer and not deal with you according to your folly."* God used Job's prayers in dealing with Eliphaz and his two friends. God wanted to forgive Eliphaz and his two friends, but Job had to pray.

We read in 1 John 5:16: *If anyone sees his brother commit a sin ... he should pray and God will give him life.* If anyone *sees* his brother committing a sin – this means, be on the alert, take responsibility for those in the world around you and if you see something that is wrong, pray. If we pray then, God will answer.

In answer to prayer God will forgive the person's sins.

James 5:16 reads: *The prayer of a righteous man is powerful and effective.* It can also be translated as: "Prayer is powerful in the way it works, it works powerfully." This means that the prayer of the righteous can accomplish or achieve something or bring it to an end. Something changes when the righteous pray. This is part of the meaning of "to rule". Through our prayers we reign, we rule, we keep watch over the earth and we protect it. Through our prayers the kingdom of God is built and the Evil One is forced to retreat.

Nobody prayed, therefore ...

In Ezekiel 22 we read of a city (Jerusalem) where the rulers enriched themselves, the priests did not live holy lives anymore, the officials made dishonest profits, the prophets proclaimed lies and the people oppressed, murdered and robbed one another. When God saw this, He looked for someone to pray for the city.

Once again God seeks the human being to come between, to pray, to rule over the earth, to take responsibility for what happens here and to act as God's representative. In Isaiah 59:16 we read that the Lord said He was appalled that no one intervened. God was amazed that no one acted as intercessor, that no one stood in the gap.

In the Old Testament the priests in particular, were the ones who represented God; who stood between God and the people and who talked with both God and the people. In the New Testament, when 1 Peter 2:9 calls us a "royal priesthood", it means that we should reign as kings, and as priests represent humankind by means of intercession before the throne.

7

Rule with Christ

We are God's representatives

What was God's original intention with humankind? We read it in various scriptures. Genesis 1:26 reads: *"Let us make man in our image, in our likeness, and let them rule ... "* In Psalm 8:4-6 we read: *...what is man that you are mindful of him, the son of man that you care for him? You made him a little lower than the heavenly beings and crowned him with glory and honor. You made him ruler over the works of your hands; you put everything under his feet.* In Psalm 115:16 the following is said: *The highest heavens belong to the Lord, but the earth he has given to man.* The Hebrew word *nathan,* which is translated in this verse as "given", can be more accurately translated as "assigned". In other words, the earth has been assigned to us human beings as the territory for which we are responsible.

What is the responsibility that the Lord gave the human

being (Adam) toward the earth which was assigned to him? We find this in Psalm 8:6: the human being had to rule over the earth. The Hebrew word *mashal*, used here means to rule, reign, dominion, govern. Adam (and thus humankind) was appointed by God to work the earth and care for it. The words "care for" are from the Hebrew word *shamar*, which literally means to protect, to guard. This is the root word for the concept "watchman", which is used often in the Bible. Adam was appointed as a watchman or guardian of the earth.

Adam had to represent God by operating as God's representative or manager of the earth. He had to be mediator, go-between or representative. What is the definition of a representative? It is a substitute, an agent, someone who can speak and act with authority on behalf of another, in that person's own interest. This is what Adam, and humankind, had to do: to talk and act on behalf of God. This does not mean removed from God, indiscriminately or in his own power. No, a representative has definite limitations, but he also has a distinct mandate and commission; authority which he is granted by the person he or she represents.

The human being is an image of God

What does this representative look like; this person that God appointed to rule over the earth? Genesis 1:27 says that the human being was created in the image of God. The Hebrew word is *tselem,* which is the root for the word "shadow" and can be translated as "illusion, likeness, resemblance, a representation, phantom". God created a representative for Himself that creates the illusion that the person looks like God! An illusion is a specific impression which is created, but if you look closer, you see that your eyes have misled you. When creation looked at Adam, he (humankind) had to remind them of God. If someone should see Adam (humankind), such a person could call out, "For a moment I thought I saw God, but it is only Adam." God's intention was something like this when he made the human being.

Look at Genesis 1:26, that says we are created in the image, the likeness of God. The Hebrew word, which is here translated as image or likeness, is *demuwth*, which is from the root *damah* and means "to compare". *Demuwth* can be translated as "in accordance with, resemblance, model, similar, like." When God created the human being in his image, He created someone who, at least in some respects, could be compared to Him or who resembled Him. Psalm 8:5 puts it like this: *You made him a little lower than the heavenly beings and crowned him with glory and honor.* God makes humankind in his image and goes on to crown him with heavenly glory as well.

Crowned with glory and honour

God crowns us with glory and honour. The two Hebrew words used here are *kabowd*, which is translated as "glory" and *hadar,* which is translated as "honour". The basic meaning of *kabouwd* is "heavy, weighty" and is directly connected with the concept of authority. It also has the meaning of "excellence or majesty". The word *hadar* also means "dominion, authority". When God crowns humankind with honour and glory, we are God's representatives and He gives us the authority to rule over the earth. We are supposed to be in control of the earth, which has been entrusted to us.

In 1 Corinthians 11:7 we read: *... he* [the man] *is the image and glory of God.* The Greek words here translated as "image" and "glory", are *eikon* and *doxa*, which have the same basic meaning as Genesis 1:26-27 and Psalm 8:6. The concept "to recognise" is built into the word *doxa.* When humankind is described as the glory of God, it means that God can be recognised in the human being. This does not mean that a human being is God, but that God can be recognised in his representative, the human being. This was God's intention when He created humankind.

Adam's mandate

Let us attempt to summarise what has been said thus far:
God made Adam (humankind) his representative.

- Adam (humankind) that God created, looks like God, is similar to God. The human being is not God, but he is the image of God, he creates the illusion that creation can think he is God.
- Adam (humankind) looks so much like God and is crowned by God with honour and glory so that he can represent God and that God can be recognised in humankind's presence.
- God assigned the earth to Adam (humankind) to rule over it. Adam was God's manager; he had the mandate from God to rule over the earth, to work it, to care for it.
- Adam was also instructed to protect the earth, to guard it. Adam (humankind) was appointed watchman over the earth.

The important conclusion of this discussion is this: *The condition of the earth, what happens here, is the responsibility of Adam and his descendants.*

Adam loses his mandate

Adam had the mandate to represent God and to rule over the earth. This mandate was assigned to Adam and his descendants. But things went horribly wrong: because of Adam's disobedience to God he gave the mandate to rule over the earth to Satan.

Together with this, he also relinquished his honour and glory, the majesty with which God clothed him. The earth that was assigned to Adam, now fell into the hands of Satan. Because of the Fall, Satan now ruled the earth. This is what Satan says to Jesus in Luke 4:6-7: *"I will give you all their authority and splendor, for it has been given to me, and I can give it to anyone I want to. So if you worship me, it will all be yours."*

Many believe Satan is telling a lie here. I am not convinced of that. Jesus does not question Satan's pronouncement that the authority and majesty of the earth belong to him, neither the fact that it was given to him. Who gave him the authority and majesty? No one but Adam! And this happened at the Fall of man.

In the Gospel of John Jesus Himself three times calls Satan "the prince of this world" (John 12:31; 14:30; 16:11). This means that the authority and mandate that Adam had to rule over the earth, belonged to Satan at that stage.

The mandate is reinstated

God's intention was to use humankind to represent Him on earth. He stands by this decision. What must God now do to take this mandate from the hand of Satan and give it back to humankind?

The price to win back this mandate was the incarnation or Jesus coming to earth in a human form, Jesus the Son of God. Humankind was still the key; Jesus still wished to work and take command on earth through humankind. That is why Jesus had to come to earth in a human form. Through the first Adam, sin came into the world, humankind lost his honour and glory and also his mandate to rule over the earth. Through the second Adam, this is Jesus, God reinstated the honour and glory of the human being and reassigned to him/her the mandate to rule, to reign and to be watchman.

This is precisely what Romans 5:17 tells us: *... and how much more will those who receive God's abundant provision of grace and of the gift of righteousness reign in life through the one man, Jesus Christ.* It is clear that the reference here is to people who, after receiving the gift of righteousness, in other words who have been redeemed from their sins and have been born again through the Spirit of God, will *reign* with Christ. Jesus' death on the cross, whereby He paid the full price for the sins and unrighteousness of humankind, gained the victory over Satan and through this, the mandate to rule over the earth was reassigned to humankind. Once again the commission is given to humankind, and in the New Testament, to the church (which consists of people), to *reign* over the earth and to be God's representatives again.

It is however, important that we as human beings now *reign* through Jesus Christ. In our commitment to Him we *reign.* Every promise in the New Testament is only valid in Christ Jesus.

8

Jesus as Intercessor

Jesus' ministry of intercession

The human being's deepest need is for someone to act as mediator between God and us. This is exactly what Jesus came to do – He came to act as mediator/intercessor between God and us. By means of his intercession, Jesus achieved reconciliation between God and humanity. What Jesus came to do is precisely what the Latin verb *intercedo* describes. The word intercession has two important aspects. Both of them are clearly mirrored in that which Jesus came to do on earth.

What Jesus did, was firstly, to *come between, go between, obstruct in coming between, to act as mediator.* Isaiah 53:12 puts it like this: *... for he bore the sins of many, and made intercession* [intercedo] *for the transgressors.*

The act of intercession also has a second aspect. Intercession can also mean *taking over or accepting co-responsibility/*

liability for someone else's debt. This is why Jesus' ministry can be defined as intercession. Jesus came to stand between God and human beings to ward off the judgment of God. He accepted responsibility for our guilt or debt and that is why He called upon us as Christians to come and stand in that position with Him.

Jesus paid the price for the sins of the world on the cross, and from this perfect sacrifice He calls upon us to approach God – to come to the Father as intercessors and to plead with the Father for the people by virtue of this perfect sacrifice. Thus we stand before the throne of grace as intercessors and plead for mercy and grace on the grounds of Jesus' death of atonement. It is very important to understand that we cannot accept co-responsibility for the sins of the world. This could be done by Christ only. What we can however do, is to come and stand before the Father in the Name of Jesus Christ and pray for the people *by virtue of Jesus' intercessory work on the cross.*

This is the work of the intercessor: not to try to be mediator himself/herself, but to plead with the Father by virtue of Christ's work as Mediator.

Gethsemane was intercession

Gethsemane was the most profound point of Jesus' ministry of intercession on earth; Golgotha was the result. In Gethsemane Jesus stood before the Father for the sins of the world. There He intervened, interceded for us, met with God.

Let us go back for a moment to the Latin word *intercedo.* The word is a compound of two Latin words: *inter,* which means *between, involved* or *intervene,* and *cedere,* which means *to go, to move, to pay the price (the price of the action of being a go-between).* When Jesus prays to the Father in Gethsemane, intervenes, intercedes, He goes to stand between God the

Father and the people and pays the price for the fact that He is the go-between. We read of his suffering, to the extent that his sweat was mixed with blood, that an angel had to support Him. Jesus says in Matthew 26:38: *"My soul is overwhelmed with sorrow to the point of death."* This was the price he paid for praying that the Father would grant salvation for sinners. The result of Jesus' intercession in Gethsemane was Golgotha, where He paid with his life for interceding for the world. The curse that was on us, came upon Him because He acted as Intercessor.

In Gethsemane Jesus calls upon the disciples to pray with Him (Matt 26:38 etc). Jesus wrestles with the Father, He struggles with the will of God. He prays that the Father will take "this cup" from Him if possible. In verse 38 Jesus says, *"My soul is overwhelmed with sorrow."* He was standing in the breach before the Father for the sins of the world, but the violence of sin was becoming such a heavy burden on Him that it literally began to suffocate Him. There in Gethsemane Jesus intervened for us with the Father as the great Intercessor and He gained the victory. For this victory Jesus had to lay down his life. He did not lose his life only on the cross. Already in Gethsemane Jesus gave up his life. And because He laid down his life for us, He paid the full price for the world's sins.

Jesus wrestled with his Father. He won the victory because he did not love his life, because no price was too high to reconcile humankind with his Father.

We can learn various lessons on intercession from Jesus' intercession in Gethsemane:

1. There must be grace and mercy in intercession; you need to be able to put yourself in the place of those you are praying for. In a certain sense you take their place before the throne of God and plead with God for the sake of their sins, distress, anxiety or whatever their needs might be.
2. Intercession does not involve my mind only; it also involves

my heart, my feelings. The fact that Jesus interceded for the sins of the world, caused Him great distress. It was so intense that drops of blood-sweat formed on his brow. The price of pleading for another's life is wrestling with God, tears and sorrow.

3. Jesus paid a price for intercession in Gethsemane. He died in the process, laid down his life; the seed fell into the ground and died – and only then it bore fruit. Many of us do not want to pray, because prayer asks that we die to self, to our interests, ambitions, dreams, comfort etcetera. Jesus' intercession in Gethsemane literally cost Him his life. But because he laid down his life, we were given life.
4. In Gethsemane Jesus, as the Son of God, came to us and asked us as humans to watch and pray with Him. He did not do it without good reason. He wanted to teach his disciples, already at that stage, that the Father makes use of people in the salvation of people. Jesus knew how powerful the intercession of the three disciples would be, what it would be worth if they would pray with Him. He is in heaven now and is still searching for intercessors to work with Him.
5. Gethsemane was about the sins of the world, a lost world. Intercession is about the brokenness of people and the world and the fact that they are lost. Intercessors often stand in "Gethsemane" when they pray for the salvation, redemption and deliverance of others.
6. Intercession bids us to keep watch – this is not the same as praying. To keep watch is to guard against danger, to take note of need, to be prepared any minute to be the go-between. In Gethsemane Jesus calls directly upon his disciples to watch, and He regards watching and praying as part and parcel of each other.

Jesus' continued ministry of intercession

Jesus had a ministry of three, maximum three and a half years on earth. During this period he preached, schooled his disciples, performed miracles and healed many sick. After that He was crucified, buried, He was raised from the dead and ascended into heaven. His work on earth was finished. A logical question would be: What is Jesus doing now at the right hand of the Father?

The answer is very clear and we find it in three passages from Scripture in particular:

- Romans 8:34: *"He is seated at the right hand of God, He intercedes for us."*
- Hebrews 7:25: *"Therefore he is able to save completely those who come to God through him, because he always lives to intercede for them."*
- Hebrews 9:24: "... [Jesus Christ] *entered heaven itself, now to appear for us in God's presence."*

The Bible is very clear about it that Jesus Christ acts as intercessor, there where He sits at the right hand of God in his transfigured form.

Intercession is the work that Jesus has been occupying Himself with for more or less the past 2000 years. His ministry on earth lasted maximum three and a half years (preaching, healings, miracles, teaching, etc.) but for the last 2000 years He has already been busy with intercession.

Let us consider this. I presume that Jesus, after ascending to heaven, would keep Himself occupied with the most effective work possible to ensure that what happened on the cross of Calvary had maximal effect – that lost sinners would be redeemed from their sin forever. Jesus chose the ministry of intercession Himself. It is of the utmost importance that this fact will not escape us. Let us become followers of Jesus in the ministry of intercession by means of intercessory prayer.

The result of Jesus' *paga* with the Father

Remember that the word *paga* has the basic meaning of *a meeting*. Jesus' work as Intercessor was meeting with God. The cross was Jesus' meeting with the Father. In this meeting, Jesus came to stand between humans and God and He met God. He took the guilt of humankind onto Him, took responsibility for it and made Himself answerable to our sin and unrighteousness. The result was that He succeeded in reconciling us with God. Reconciliation took place. The Mediator succeeded in his mediation.

In his book *Intercessory Prayer*, Dutch Sheets describes this meeting as follows:

- Compassion *meets* Judgment;
- Righteousness *meets* Sin;
- Light *meets* Darkness;
- Humility *meets* Pride;
- Love *meets* Hate;
- Life *meets* Death;
- The cursed One on the cross *meets* the curse that originated at the tree;
- The Resurrected One *meets* the finality of death.

In this meeting God gains, in Jesus Christ, the victory over all the minuses in life. Satan is conquered, Sin is conquered. The judgment and vengeance of God are "conquered". Darkness is conquered. Christ's mediation has released God's grace and compassion, because He, as the Lamb without blemish, brought the perfect offer of Himself for our sins. With this the judgment and vengeance of God were conquered and the grace and compassion of God could start working.

9

The intercessionary "trinity"

Intercession is a spiritual act in which three parties are involved: Jesus Christ at the right hand of the Father, the Holy Spirit, who lives in the intercessor, and the intercessor himself/herself. In intercession these three parties work together. The intercessor cannot do the work of intercession without the Holy Spirit and Jesus Christ. In the following paragraphs I pay attention to the role of each partaker.

The intercessor

The mandate of the intercessor

The intercessor has a *right and a mandate to go to God,* to appear before God's throne. What gives him the right? Jesus is the key – Jesus earned this right on the cross. There was a day in the history of humankind that God's Son paid the price for the sins of the world, when Jesus Christ broke the curse of sin over humankind. He paid the full price and called out on the cross, *"Tetelestai"*, which means "It is finished", "The price has been paid." The minute that Jesus cried out this word (John 19:30), the curtain of the temple tore (Mark 15:37-39). This means that by his death He opened up the entrance to the Holy of holies. Now we can go directly to the throne of God in prayer. We no more need to bring sacrifices and approach God only by means of the mediation of priests. Jesus is the sacrifice and He passed through the curtain Himself, to the throne of God, as a result of the perfect sacrifice that He brought. *Now we too have the right to approach the throne of God.* Hebrews 4:16 says that we can approach the throne of grace with confidence so that we can be helped in our time of need.

In addition, we have a commission from God, a command from God to pray. Think of passages like 1 Timothy 2:1-2; Philippians 4:5-7; Matthew 7:7-11 and others where we are called upon to pray. In other words, two things give us the right to pray: the price that Jesus paid on the cross and also the fact that God the Father invites us to pray, but even more so because the Father also gives us a command to pray.

Jesus Christ

1. The cross is our only valid argument

   Our intercessory prayers are merely the continuation of Jesus' act of intercession that reached its climax on the cross. This, to me, is the single most important principle that every intercessor should understand. When we pray as intercessors, we do so only by virtue of the intercessory work of Christ and on no other grounds.

- God does not listen to our prayers because of our seriousness, although it is important to be serious.

- God doesn't listen to our prayers because we use the correct words, the right expressions and the right terminology, although it is important that we pray correctly.
- God doesn't listen to us because He answered our prayers in the past, although this gives us faith and confidence because we know God answers prayer.
- God doesn't answer our prayers because we pray well, pray for hours on end or are spiritually mature.
- God listens to our prayers because there was a day, about 2000 years ago, when Jesus Christ, the Perfect Intercessor, paid the ransom for our sins by means of an act of intercession on the cross of Calvary.

2. Intercession is rooted in God's grace and compassion
Thus the act of intercession is rooted in the death and resurrection of Jesus Christ, because the cross and resurrection of Jesus reveal God's *grace and mercy to us.* Grace is to receive what we do *not* deserve and mercy is *not* to receive what we *do* deserve.

When the intercessor prays, he appeals to the grace and mercy of God as these were revealed in Jesus' redeeming death on the cross. The intercessor has no authority of his/her own. There is nothing in the intercessor that will move God to answer him/her, except when the intercessor approaches the Father in the Name of Jesus Christ and asks in Jesus' Name that God will do something. Jesus promises in John 14:13-14 that what we ask in his Name, we will be given. Seven times in the New Testament we read the command: pray in Jesus' Name (John 14:13, 14; 1 John 3:21-22).

What does it mean to pray in Jesus' Name? When I pray, I appeal to God's grace and mercy. When I pray for someone, I call out to God: "Father, You are a merciful and gracious God. Jesus has already paid for the sin and redemption of X. On the grounds of the cross I appeal to your grace and compassion. I ask that You will be merciful and gracious."

Answer to prayer does not depend on how much we have grown spiritually or how mature we are, but whether we know and understand how to pray in Jesus' Name.

When I pray in Jesus' Name, I confess that I have not contributed anything towards the salvation of any person or towards reconciliation between God and people, but that I am completely dependent on Jesus' death of atonement on the cross. God the Father doesn't hear us because we are good at praying, or pray in the correct way or use a specific formula, but He listens to hear if we know how to plead that He will hear us *for Jesus' sake*.

We have too many so-called prayer experts today. There is no such thing as a "black belt" intercessor. There are people who think they have discovered the secret of intercession and prayer warfare, that they are on a higher level than other believers, but they don't understand that the only grounds for access to the Father and the only way to be certain of an answer to prayer is found in the Name of Jesus Christ. When I as intercessor stand before God in prayer, I approach Him only in the Name of Jesus and on the grounds of the grace and compassion of God, which are at our disposal through the cross of Jesus Christ.

3. Because God is gracious and merciful

God is a merciful and gracious God. The power of the gospel is the grace and mercy of God. The grace and mercy of God as expressed in Jesus' death on the cross make the Christian religion unique.

And it is precisely by virtue of the grace and mercy of God that the intercessor may approach God. The intercessor has no other mandate or right to approach God. God shows his grace and mercy by the death of his Son. The intercessors come to the Father on the grounds of John 3:16, the fact that God so loved the world that He gave his only Son so that whoever believes in Him will not perish, but have eternal life.

The intercessor has no lawful right to plead with God and to ask that God will avert his judgment and save the person for whom he is praying, except on the grounds of what happened on the cross. The cross is the intercessor's first and last argument when he calls out to God. The intercessor never comes to God on the grounds that he/she is something or someone, and neither because God answered prayers in the past, or because the intercessor is sincere or prays fervently. We are not answered because we pray for hours on end or because we are humble or because we have great faith.

The Holy Spirit

1. Our Helper in intercession
   In Romans 8:26-27 the Bible teaches us that God the Father gives us the Holy Spirit as our Helper in intercession. He intercedes for us with the Father with groans that words cannot express. Sometimes we don't know how to pray. It is then that Holy Spirit comes and "sighs" or "groans" before God for us. The Holy Spirit also comes and presents our prayers to God in the correct way. In Jude verse 20 and Ephesians 6:18 we are encouraged to pray in the Spirit – that is to pray under the guidance of the Spirit and with his help. Galatians 4:6 teaches us that the Spirit of God is sent into our hearts and He calls out, "Abba Father." It is only through the workings of the Holy Spirit that we can really call out "Abba Father" and that we can pray within God's will.
2. The Holy Spirit and prayer burdens
   Prayer burdens can have one of four sources:
   (a) Self
   Often our prayer burdens are our own needs or desires or our own feelings of sympathy for others. It is often these burdens

that wear us down spiritually and tire us so that we become totally exhausted. Outwardly, these burdens may appear to be very spiritual, but the fact that they originate in the self is the cause that God does not provide the spiritual strength for these. The "emergency" character of these prayer burdens, and the fact that they can even have spiritual qualities and are directed at the needs of others, make that Christians are easily misled.

(b) Other people

Prayer burdens can also come from other people. Believers and even unbelievers can sometimes force a prayer burden on us with: "Will you please pray for me about this or that matter? I am counting on your intercession." My answer to such people is usually, "I undertake to pray for you as often as the Holy Spirit reminds me to pray for you." Don't promise to pray if you are not convinced that the Holy Spirit has laid it upon you to pray for that person, irrespective of how urgent, noble or creditworthy the case may be.

(c) The devil

The third source of prayer burdens is the devil. Satan can very easily come and dish up prayer burdens for you. Such prayer burdens can be recognised because they often unload a big, heavy burden on you and lead to guilt feelings if you forget to pray. The burden weighs you down and you do not really wish to pray for the matter.

(d) The Holy Spirit

All three types of the abovementioned burdens are wrong. We must receive our burdens from the Holy Spirit – He must show us for whom, when and how long we should pray for a particular matter. God the Father only provides power, wisdom, guidance and perseverance for burdens that are given by the Spirit of God.

As Christians we should attempt never to do things in reaction to something that happens. This is true of intercession as well. A sports council once approached me to use their sports grounds a certain weekend and hold a succession of services there. The motivation for their request was that an extremist group wanted the stadium that particular weekend for their services. A wise spiritual leader of the city said to me, "If you now go and present a succession of services it will be a reaction to something the devil wants to do. As Christians we should only be mobilised on God's command, never as a reaction to a crisis, or a need that exists or arises." This is wise advice that also holds good for intercessors. Many intercessors notice an emergency and immediately start praying for it. It could be dangerous to do that. Why? Because the emergency "forces" you to pray and you don't first find out from God how you must pray for it. If we have to react to the need of the world around us all the time, we would never sleep and we would be busy praying for emergency and crisis situations 24 hours a day. That is why it is so important to find out from God what we must pray for, how we must pray for it and when we can stop praying for the matter. If we do this, our intercession will be "initiatives" that are born of the Spirit of God and not reactions to human needs and crises caused by the devil. 1 John 5:4 says that every person who is born of the Spirit (and we could add to that all things born of God), conquer the world. The things that are not born of God cannot conquer the world.

Prayers that are born of God will gain the "victory", but prayers that are not born of God, will not gain a victory.

10

Can God change his mind?

A sheep farmer who influenced the future of a nation

Amos was a sheep farmer from Tekoa. He lived in a time of material prosperity, political stability and apparent religious activity, but it was a time of serious spiritual degeneration and malpractice on the social-ethical side. In Amos God found a man that He could use; through Amos God could talk to the people about their sins and Amos could talk to Him about the sins of the people.

In Amos 7:1 we read how the Lord pronounced judgement over Israel: *This is what the Sovereign Lord showed me: He was preparing swarms of locusts ...* What was Amos' reaction? He could do one of two things. He could say that God is sovereign and would not change his mind and leave it at that. But Amos chose a second way – He called upon God! Look carefully what is written: *When they had stripped the land clean, I cried out, "Sovereign Lord, forgive! How can Jacob survive? He is so small! So the Lord relented, "This will not happen," the Lord said* (Amos 7:2-3). It is almost unbelievable. God pronounced judgment, but because Amos stood in the breach and pleaded with God, God changed his mind and judgment was averted.

In Amos 7:4-7 God once again announced judgment over Israel. Once again Amos prayed and it is written in verse 6: *So the Lord relented. "This will not happen either ..."* This means that God changes his mind – and it is directly related to intercession.

Abraham's aparent failure

There is an amazing example of intercession in the life of Abraham. In Genesis 18:16-33 we read how Abraham intercedes for the cities Sodom and Gomorrah. There are many lessons in this for us as intercessors.

In the first half of Genesis 18 we read that the Lord came to Abraham. Take note: God came to Abraham. The Lord decided that He would not hide from Abraham what He was planning to do with Sodom and Gomorrah (Gen 18:16-19). Abraham's reaction was exactly what God wanted it to be: Abraham started talking to the Lord about these two cities, he acted as intercessor. Intercession originates in the heart of God. It is God who is working in us to will as well as work, says Philippians 2:13. It is not that we are so spiritual to intercede for others; no, it is God who works it in our hearts through the Holy Spirit to intercede for others.

Abraham started talking to God: "Lord, what if there are fifty righteous people in the city?" Abraham goes on pleading: 45, 40, 30, 20 and 10. When Abraham came to ten righteous people, he stopped talking and praying. Genesis 18:33 is now important. In our current translation we read that God had now finished speaking to Abraham and that He left and Abraham returned home. There is however strong testimony that this verse must be read in reverse. The most original sources say: *When Abraham had finished speaking to God, he turned around and went away.* Thus the difference is that currently the verse reads that God turned around and went away, and not that Abraham turned around and left. If we accept the older verse, it means that the Lord was waiting for Abraham to continue praying, but that his courage most probably failed him.

Could Abraham have come down in the number of righteous people so that Sodom and Gomorrah would have been saved? Is there any Scriptural evidence? I think so. There is a key in Jeremiah 5:1: *"Go up and down in the streets of Jerusalem, look around and consider, search through her squares. If you can find but one person who deals honestly and seeks the truth, I will forgive this city."* Here the Lord would have been satisfied with but one righteous person to save the city. God would have changed his mind, would have revoked his judgment, if He had found one righteous person. I believe that Abraham could have asked God for one righteous person and God would have heard him. Was there one righteous person in these two godless cities? Yes, there was at least one: Lot (2 Pet 2:7). Did Abraham succeed in his intercession or did he fail? He failed in the sense that the two cities were destroyed. But there is something else that we need to focus on. Lot and his two daughters were saved from this destruction. Lot's eldest daughter had a son that she called Moab (Gen 19:37). Of Moab's descendants, Ruth was one, a Moabite that eventually married Boaz. She was the great-grandmother of David and later Jesus was a descendant of David (Matt 1:5-6). The essence is this: Although Sodom and Gomorrah were destroyed, Lot and his two daughters were saved by Abraham's intercession and almost 2 000 years later Jesus Christ, the Saviour of the world, was born of the descendants of Lot. Is this not tremendous? Abraham's intercession in Genesis 18 can be directly linked to the birth of Christ 2000 years later, which made salvation possible for all of humanity.

Thus Abraham's victory was bigger than his apparent defeat. He failed with Sodom and Gomorrah, but through his intercession the Saviour, Christ Jesus, came to the earth.

The unwilling prophet

In Jonah 3 we read that the prophet Jonah pronounced the judgment of God over the city of Nineveh. When the inhabitants of Nineveh heard it, they humbled themselves, prayed and repented. God heard them, changed his mind and spared the city. This is what we read in Jeremiah 18:7-8: *"If at any time I announce that a nation or kingdom is to be uprooted, torn down and destroyed, and if that nation I warned repents of its evil, then I will relent and not inflict on it the disaster I had planned.* God can change his mind – but then the people must humble themselves before Him and return to God.

"You can erase my name from your book"

In Exodus 32 we read that God changed his mind. The people defied God and worshipped a golden calf. God was angry and decided to destroy his people. Moses prayed to God and God changed his mind. The Lord says in Exodus 32:10: *"Now leave me alone so that my anger may burn against them and that I may destroy them.* In Exodus 32:14 however, we read: *Then the Lord relented and did not bring on his people the disaster he had threatened.* What happened between verse 10 and verse 14? We read about this in the rest of Exodus 32 and in Deuteronomy 9. In Exodus 32:32 we read that Moses prayed: *"But now please forgive their sin – but if not, then blot me out of the book you have written."* The attitude revealed here by Moses points to that which Christ would do more than a thousand years later on the cross. Moses was willing to give his life so that the people of Israel could be saved. God could not accept this offer, because it would not have been sufficient. Only Christ could bring that offer. But God saw Moses' attitude and listened to him. We read in Psalm 106:23: *So he said he would destroy them – had not Moses, his chosen one, stood in the breach before him to keep his wrath from destroying them.* Also in this case, the judgment was already announced, but because there was an intercessor who was desperate and who called upon God with his whole being, God changed his mind.

Intercessors swim against the current when others go with the flow

Intercession is often a lonely road. On this road few people understand you (this doesn't mean you should behave in such a way that people don't understand you). Often intercessors appear to be somewhat eccentric because they communicate in a spiritual dimension. There is a dimension of faith to see the unseen, to hear the prophetic word and the promptings of the Holy Spirit. It is there where I take God at his Word and where the promises of the Lord are greater realities than the physical, visible circumstances around me. Intercessors swim against the current when others go with the flow. Intercessors believe in God when everybody else has lost faith and hope.

Elijah walked this solitary road for many years, and so did Elisha. This was the daily bread of the prophets of yesteryear. Jesus, our eternal Intercessor, walked this solitary road when He prayed alone at night and all through the night. On occasion God locked Daniel in alone for 21 days, cut off from the world.

11

The paradox of intercession

What is a paradox?

A paradox is a statement that appears to be absurd, illogical and contradictory. At first it does not seem to have a logical explanation. It could also be a statement that goes against the accepted opinion.

When we are busy with the kingdom of God, the principles of the kingdom of God and the way God works, we very often seem to be confronted with paradoxes. The concept *Holy Trinity* is a paradox. How can 3X1=1? Logically it is not possible. Our salvation from sin is 100% God's responsibility, and yet it is 100% our responsibility to become converted to God. It is a paradox, it does not work logically, it appears to be a contradiction.

Paul often makes use of paradoxical statements. We read in 2 Corinthians 6:8-10: *... through glory and dishonor, bad report* *and good report; genuine, yet regarded as impostors; known, yet regarded as unknown; dying and yet we live on; beaten and yet not killed; sorrowful, yet always rejoicing; poor, yet making many rich; having nothing, and yet possessing everything.*

There are many paradoxes, also where prayer is concerned. In the following paragraphs I would like to talk about a few paradoxes, apparent contradictions, in intercession.

Paradoxes in intercession

Paradox 1: It is our task to pray and God's task to answer. God "uses" the same prayer to save and to judge.

Too often it happens that we pray, but at the same time we want to prescribe to God how He should answer. God is sovereign. He invites us to pray. It pleases Him that we pray. He wants to listen to our prayers, but there can never be a point where we can tell God how to answer. When it is said that we must be specific when we pray, it does not mean we can prescribe to God what He should answer. Neither does it mean that I can ask God directly for a specific answer. I may ask, but the answer will always be God's answer.

God is more interested in our character than in giving us things. God is in the industry of character building. God is not seated on his throne in order to entertain us with miracles. God is capable of raising the dead (and He does it to this day). He can heal the sick (and daily He heals thousands of people), He can provide for our daily needs (and He takes care of 5, 8 billion people every day), but God also has priorities and He also has a will.

We pray and ask certain things from the Lord. God is good and answers our prayers. But because He is God, his answer is perfect and so his answer is not always what we expect it to be.

Have you ever prayed for faith? People pray and ask, "Lord,

give me greater faith." And the Lord answers us, but not supernaturally by putting two jugs of faith in our hands. Romans 5:3-5 teaches us that suffering produces perseverance and perseverance leads to greater faith. This means that when I ask God for more faith, God answers me straight away, and he gives me suffering. Because we do not understand God's spiritual principles, we are rebellious about the suffering, and in the end, we do not grow in faith.

Sometimes we pray Psalm 139 and ask the Lord to search our hearts and to see if there is any offensive way in us; we pray and tell the Lord we want to serve Him with greater dedication. God answers us and wants to give us our heart's desire, but He does it in his way, the only way that He knows will have results. 1 Peter 1:6-7 teaches us that when God wants to test how genuine our faith is He will refine us, and send many trials. James says our faith must be tested in the same way the purity of gold is tested by fire. The fire in which gold is tested is hundreds of degrees Celsius. God often places us in a furnace that is hundreds of degrees Celsius and then we think He is cruel or He has abandoned us. No, He tests our faith, He refines it. If we hold onto God, we will come out stronger on the other side.

Very often when we pray to God and ask for deliverance in a certain situation, God sends judgment as well as salvation. In Habakkuk's case God answered with judgement. In Revelation 8:1-5 and 5:8 we read that the prayers of believers are caught up in heaven in large gold basins or bowls. What is the effect of those prayers? In Revelation, chapter 6, we read that God sends judgement onto the earth. The same happens in Revelation 8 from verse 6 when the prayers and incense (v 1-5) in big gold bowls have already been offered before God on the altar. The angels then get ready and sound the trumpets. These are however trumpets that announce the beginning of new activity from heaven; judgment is passed on the people (Rev 8-12).

Look at Jeremiah's prayer. He prays that God should come

and restore the people, but God answers him and judgment upon judgement is pronounced over the people. In Jeremiah 1, he is called by God as prophet and he prays and intercedes for the people. The effect of these prayers however, is time and time again the condemnation of the Lord. This makes Jeremiah so despondent that He weeps before God and later on he does not want to prophesy the judgment of God anymore. In Jeremiah 20:9 he tells us how he tries to resist the Word of God, but that it becomes like a burning fire in him – he simply has to say what God says to him.

Another example is when Lazarus, the brother of Martha and Mary, died. In John 11 we read that he became ill. Martha and Mary sent a message to Jesus to ask Him to come so that Lazarus would not die. Then we read in John 11:5-6 that Jesus waited two days before He went to Martha and Mary. One translation says: *"Jesus loved Martha and her sister and Lazarus; [they were His dear friends] ... Therefore (even) when He heard that Lazarus was sick, He still stayed two days longer in the same place where He was."* Martha and Mary prayed and asked Jesus to come and heal Lazarus, but Jesus waited for Lazarus to die first before He went there. Why? Because He knew the heart of his Father – Lazarus' death had to bear testimony to the omnipotence of God. We as human beings only know in part and we understand only in part, but the Perfect One knows all – that is why we can approach the throne of grace with confidence and leave our prayers with God. He knows how to answer them.

Read the book Habakkuk. The prophet prays to God for the recovery of Israel. What is God's answer? In Habakkuk 1:5, God says to the prophet, *" ... I am going to do something in your days that you would not believe, even if you were told."* Habakkuk is probably excited when he hears this. Surely it could mean one thing only and that is that Israel would be restored. But God goes on to say: *"I am raising up the*

Babylonians, that ruthless and impetuous people … they are a law to themselves and promote their own honour … they all come bent on violence" (Hab 1:6-9). God answers Habakkuk, but his answer holds judgment, not deliverance. God sends judgment over the people. We pray; God answers as He wills.

Paradox 2: God gives the vision but He also determines the time of fulfilment for the vision. God answers our prayers, but He is not in a hurry.

Worldwide, the church is praying for revival. God however, wants repentance of sins and He desires that Christians will once again return to their first love. Someone put it this way: The church wants revival, God wants repentance. What is currently happening throughout the entire church of Christ? Considerable parts of the church are becoming convicted of their sin. They pray for revival, but all that is apparently happening, is that people confess their sins. This doesn't look like revival. But this is in fact the forerunner of revival. We pray for revival, but God knows He cannot give instant revival, there must first be confession of sins. The church is praying for revival, God convicts of sin.

Many people in South Africa have been praying for revival for years. Often when I tire of praying, the Spirit comes and encourages me to persist. In our instant society where we live on instant coffee, instant puddings and instant recipes, it is difficult to wait.

Sometimes we pray for a day or two and if nothing happens, we decide it is not the will of God and we stop. Others pray for a week or two, perhaps a month.

It is said of George Mueller that he started praying for five of his friends who did not know the Lord. After five years the first one repented and became converted. The second one was converted after 10 years; the third one after 25 years. Thirty eight years later someone once asked him, "Why do you keep on praying for these two friends of yours. If they have not repented after 38 years of prayer, they will certainly not do it now." Fire blazed in George Mueller's eyes when he said, "Do you think God will call on me to pray 38 years for these two men if He does not want to save them?" The fourth one repented and was converted after 50 years, and the last one was converted at George Mueller's funeral, after George had been praying for him almost 52 years. It is our task to pray, and God will answer in his own time.

I had the privilege of talking to the writer Wesley Duewel. He made this important remark: "I do not believe that the Spirit of God is playing the fool when He is calling on Christians in many countries all over the world to pray for revival. I believe that God is serious about worldwide revival."

It is God who calls upon the church to pray for revival. God however, has his own time schedule, his own seasons. God is sovereign and He determines the time and place of everything. It is in Ecclesiastes 3:1-11 that we learn there is a fixed time for everything: *There is a time ... to plant and a time to uproot ... a time to tear down and a time to build ... a time to be silent and a time to speak ...*

Someone once said: "God is almighty slow, but He is always on time." It is remarkable how the Bible teaches us to wait upon God. Time and again we are called upon in the Bible: "Be still, and know that I am God." God wants us to understand that He is in control. He will not be too late – and He is never too early.

12

Intercession is more than prayer

Acts of intercession in the Bible

Intercession is not only to pray; it is also "to do". It often entails also physical action. Intercession is not only to pray. In Numbers 25:6-13 we read about Phinehas who zealously served his God and also made atonement for the people of Israel. What exactly did Phinehas do? There was the case of the man who took a Midianite woman into the Israelite camp and before the eyes of the people of Israel behaved in a licentious manner, in this way challenging God. Phinehas took a spear, entered the tent where this Israelite and the Midianite woman were and drove the spear through both of them. God credited this to him as righteousness and the judgment of God was averted from the people. We read in Psalm 106:31: *But Phinehas stood up and intervened, and the plague was checked. This was credited to him as righteousness for endless generations to come.* The

Hebrew word for "stood up" is *palal*, which means to come between, pray. Thus Phinehas came and stood between God and the sin of these two people; in an act of intercession he prayed and also performed a physical action, and consequently God's judgment was averted from the people of Israel.

In Exodus 32:25-28 we read how a number of Levites took action and that it contributed towards the rescue of Israel. When Moses came down from the mountain and saw the people worshipping the golden calf, the Levites came to stand at Moses' side. Each one then took his sword and went criss-cross through the camp of the Israelites, killing 3000 of them. This act of the Levites bears the stamp of intercession. Because they did it, God rewarded them and this definitely contributed towards the fact that Israel was saved from the hand of the Lord.

Missionaries who go out to the mission field and live the gospel practically among the people and proclaim the Word, are at the deepest level, intercessors. Merely the act of being a missionary in a dark place bears the stamp of intercession. In that they already stand before God and plead for the salvation of people. This act of living out and proclaiming the Word among unsaved people is a forerunner of intercession, but it is also already intercession in itself. Intensive intercession in the form of prayer flows from this physical act of being a missionary.

All who go and stand between God and people in their sin, stand there as intercessors. There is a direct connection between intercession and reconciliation. Intercession is the ministry of reconciliation, because this is in fact the aim of intercession: to achieve reconciliation between God and people. In 2 Corinthians 5 Paul distinctly says that God gave us the ministry of reconciliation. Jesus, the Mediator, made reconciliation between God and people possible. What is Jesus doing currently, now, today, 2000 years after Calvary? He intercedes for us with the Father. Why? So that God and people can be reconciled.

Acts of intercession in the history of the church

In the following few paragraphs I give two examples of Christians whose lives were acts of intercession. There are, however, many more. In our time there are people like Billy Graham (evangelist preacher to the multitudes, Richard Bonnke (*Christ for All Nations),* George Verwer (founder of *Operation Mobilisation),* Loren Cunningham (founder of *Youth with a Mission),* Cameron Townsend (founder of Wycliffe Bible translators, David Wilkerson (*Teen Challenge),* Paul Freed (*Trans World Radio),* and many more. Then there are those from previous centuries like Andrew Murray (author, involved in mission mobilization), John Wesley (father of the Wesleyan church), William Booth (founder of the Salvation Army) and thousands of others.

William Wilberforce (1759-1834)

William Wilberforce grew up in England and at a young age he was already a member of the British parliament. At the age of 26, in 1785, Wilberforce was radically converted. He wanted to leave politics immediately and become a church minister. The well-known John Wesley wrote to him and encouraged him to stay where he was and use his influence as a Christian in the political arena.

Four years later, in 1789, Wilberforce wrote that he aimed to do two things: change legislation so that the slave-trade would be against the law, and change the complete lifestyle of the people of England. At that stage England was experiencing one of its most corrupt and darkest periods in history.

The task that Wilberforce set himself was humanly impossible. Slavery was part of the entire Western civilisation and it was unthinkable that this practice would be abolished. At the time, the financial gain from slave trading in England compared well with the USA defence force budget as it stood towards the end of the 20th century. For one man to take on such an undertaking and to think that he would put an end to slavery was simply humanly impossible.

William Wilberforce believed in God and acted as intercessor. He stood between the slaves and the British Parliament in Jesus' name. In his lifetime Wilberforce was one of the most despised people in England. People hated him, taunted him, insulted and rejected him for his point of view on slavery. He was even physically assaulted. His friends rejected him and most people regarded him as a hopelessly naïve extremist. He had the support of a tiny group of members of parliament.

In 1834, after more than 44 years of strife in parliament, slavery was abolished. A few days after this law was passed, Wilberforce went into a coma and died shortly afterwards.

What William Wilberforce did, was intercession, an act of intercession. Often he stood before the throne of God and interceded for the slaves and the British people and the British Parliament. At other times he endured the abuse of people when he fought the cause against slavery in the British parliament in a physical act of intercession. God looked for a man to stand in the breach for the slaves – God found William Wilberforce.

William Carey: Father of the modern mission movement

Mission scientists regard William Carey as the "father of the modern mission movement." He was from the lower middle class and a shoemaker.

On occasion he stood up during a consistorial meeting and made an appeal that the congregation and the church as a whole should take the gospel to the heathens. The chairman of the meeting silenced him with the words: "Young man, if God wants to save the heathens He will do so without you, or our help. Please sit down." However, Carey read his Bible and what the church of the time said was just not in agreement with Matthew 28:19-20 and the Great Commission to do missionary work.

By 1792 William Carey, at that stage a church leader, founded together with 11 other leaders, the first mission movement. A few months later, in June 1793, he boarded a ship to India where he died 40 years later without ever seeing England again.

Carey settled in India, in the city which is currently known as Calcutta, and worked there for forty years. His goal was to translate the Bible into Indian languages and to establish an Indian church. It took seven years before he saw the first convert. Twenty years after his arrival in India, in 1814, Carey had translated the New Testament into 15 languages. By 1834, the year in which Carey died, he had translated the complete Bible into six languages and the New Testament was available in 34 different Indian languages. In addition, Carey also planted 26 Indian churches.

His motto was: "Attempt great things for God, expect great things from God." At another occasion Carey said the following about himself: "If you want to remember me, remember me as a plodder for God."

What Carey did, was an act of intercession. He stood between the Indian nation and God's judgment; he prayed and "did." From Carey, the shoemaker's ministry, the modern mission movement was born. Today, 200 years later, we look back and we cannot believe that there was a time in which the church did not understand that Matthew 28:19-20 literally means that we must take the gospel to those who have never heard it.

Every missionary and every mission mobilizer who is involved in the spreading of the gospel, and those who make the gospel accessible to the unsaved and the unreached, are busy praying and "doing" in an act of intercession. May God our Father, the Lord to whom the harvest belongs, literally *force* tens of thousands of new workers to go out and take the gospel to the unsaved. (In Matthew 9:38 the word "send" is used, but the Greek word here *(ekballo)* could be better translated as "drive out, force out.") Thus, new workers must be forced to go out and take the gospel to the unsaved.

13

Intercessory worship

We read in Revelation 5:8: *Each one* [of the 24 elders] *had a harp and they were holding golden bowls full of incense, which are the prayers of the saints.* Take note of the words *harp* and *golden bowls.* Here we read a description of how the 24 elders knelt down, put their crowns before God and honoured God with worship and intercession. The golden bowls in heaven are used to gather the prayers/intercession of the believers (Rev 5:8; 8:4). Hebrews 7:25 teaches us that Jesus Christ acts as Intercessor in heaven. Jesus rules by means of intercession, his own and the intercession of believers, in an atmosphere of praise and worship. The main activity around the throne of God is worship, praise and intercession.

All genuine intercessors will confirm the importance of worship. We can however be caught up into one of two extremes: one group of Christians put the emphasis on intercession, and they are quite right, but it may never be at the expense of worship. Another group of Christians again emphasise the importance of worship, but they should remember that intercession also has a rightful place. In fact, Jesus spends his time in heaven to stand before God on our behalf, to plead for us with God – in other words He is busy with intercession.

Perhaps we should rather talk about *intercessory worship,* considering the verse in Revelation 5:8. One cannot go without the other. Worship leads to intercession and intercession leads to worship. The one flows from the other. Whoever starts with worship, will inevitably also start with intercession and whoever starts with intercession will inevitably worship God. We should not try to separate the two concepts, although we can differentiate. The one cannot do without the other.

Many Christians who feel strongly about worship, quote 2 Chronicles 20:21: *After consulting the people, Jehoshaphat appointed men to sing to the Lord and to praise him for the splendor of his holiness as they went out at the head of the army, saying: "Give thanks to the Lord, for his love endures forever."* Here the Levites accompanied the army with praise and worship. Other Christians who feel strongly about intercession, quote the same 2 Chronicles 20, but emphasise verses 3-4: *Alarmed, Jehoshaphat resolved to inquire of the Lord, and he proclaimed a fast for all Judah. The people of Judah came together to seek help from the Lord; indeed, they came from every town in Judah to seek him.* Here we have a distinct reference to intercession.

Intercessors cannot understand how worshippers can concentrate on worship and praise all the time while there is so much sin, so many lost people and the judgement of God hovers over people. Worshippers cannot understand how intercessors can plead and intercede continuously while God is so great and praiseworthy.

Let us not play intercession and worship off against each other. Let us combine these two facets of prayer. God combines them in the Bible. It is the same Lord who gave us both forms of prayer. One is not more important than the other. We need spiritual discernment to know when it is time for intercession and when it is time for worship.

Worship

Worship is such an important theme that a few paragraphs in a chapter cannot do justice to the matter.

A few comments will however, suffice. Since the nineteen sixties there has been a worldwide new understanding for worship in the church. But it was particularly during the nineteen eighties and nineties that this movement had a powerful breakthrough. Unfortunately it also happened that many impurities wormed their way into the process. Many vocalists and artists turned the spotlight on themselves instead of focusing their praise and worship songs on the Lord. Secondly, it started happening that many church leaders and worship teams in churches started using worship as a technique, as a special effect. Thirdly, it also happened that people were using worship for "entertainment" and in the process lost the essence of worship.

Worship is about God and God alone. In worship we lose ourselves in God. The people who worship are not hoping to find something in it for themselves. Worship does not have a hidden agenda.

It is in worship where we come to stand in the presence of God, that a meeting with God takes place. There the Lord convicts us more deeply of sin and this normally leads to confession of sin and greater commitment to God. Worship that does not lead to greater commitment to God is not true worship. But in God's presence, as I give myself anew and more passionately to God and put myself at his disposal, God gives me instructions, makes his will known to me. Through worship God teaches me what the following assignments will be and what work needs to be done. It is important to understand that worship is not a technique to find out what the Lord wants me to do. Yet the consequences of true worship are that God makes his will and his way clear to me.

There where I stand before God in worship, in complete surrender to Him, acknowledge my indescribable insignificance and stand in awe of his immeasurable greatness, of being God, He comes and reveals Himself to me afresh; He teaches me his will and gives me his instructions. These instructions include work assignments and prayer burdens (intercession).

Almost without exception, true worship leads to deeper brokenness, deeper repentance of our sins, a deeper hatred of sin, greater holiness in our walk through life. Worship that does not lead to new holiness and that does not result in people confessing their sins and bowing to the omnipotence of God, is not true worship.

Praise

Part of worship is praise. In the following paragraphs I wish to make a few comments on praise. There is power in praise. Satan hates jubilant Christians. He hates it when God is honoured. He hates it and is distraught when people ignore him and his onslaughts, and when people worship and praise God for his goodness, compassion and grace. Praise ignores Satan and honours God. Praise focuses the attention on God and the one who prays in this way brings himself/herself in a position where God is allowed to work unhindered.

Power is released on the spiritual level when believers praise and honour God. Praise awakens faith in the believer's heart, and problems, persecution and depression are diminished. Praise helps us to avert our eyes from the battle so that we see victory and our King. It breaks the chains of hopelessness, unbelief and depression in the heart of the believer. Often when we do not experience a breakthrough in prayer, it is praise that gives the victory, because praise says, "Lord, we can do nothing, but You can do everything." In praise it is all about God Himself and not about what He can give me or do for me. Time and time again believers have had to find out that victories are gained when God is praised and glorified and not when all kinds of "techniques" come into play.

In the spiritual battle against the Evil One and in prayer warfare, praise is an indispensable "weapon" for those who pray. Yes, when we are in the thick of the battle, we must lay the foundation for the final victory by means of praise. Praise is not only part of the battle plan, it is *the battle itself.* It is not something we do to thank God when the victory has already been gained. It is particularly when we are in the line of fire, and then start glorifying and praising God that the foundation is laid for victory. However, praise that is simply a technique and empty words, and that is not accompanied by faith and does not come from the heart, will have no effect.

In Isaiah 61:1-3 it says literally that we should put on the garment of praise. When we enter God's presence, we should do it with praise, wearing the garment of praise. It honours God. God delights in it.

We live in times where a spirit of heaviness has descended on many countries and many people, yes even over Christians. We must cast this off by glorifying and praising the Lord. Sometimes we need to do it with relentlessness, even if we don't really feel like doing it. We must do it irrespective of the circumstances. Fact is: God is on the throne, He is in control, He reigns, He sweeps us along in his triumphal procession. We should learn not to live according to our feelings, but according to the facts God gives us in his Word. This brings deliverance.

In Psalm 50:14 we read that praise is the offering that God wants from us. More than anything God wants us to praise Him.

And it is people who praise God who find it easy to obey Him as well. Praise without obedience to the Father is hypocrisy and has no power.

Praise has various facets. I mention only a few aspects: songs of praise, spiritual music, prayers of praise and choric dance.

There is tremendous spiritual power in song. Think of Paul and Silas in prison (Acts 16:25-26).They are in jail, in chains, but start lauding and praising God the Father. The result is an earthquake and the chains fall from their wrists. (Terry Law makes the humorous comment that when we begin to praise God, God sometimes sings along, but He sings bass, and this results in earthquakes as in Acts 16.)

Part of heaven's protocol is that we enter into God's presence with songs of praise. It often transpires from the Bible that music and song will be the most important ingredients of our heavenly activities. One of the most interesting developments the past twenty years and especially the past five to ten years, is the magnitude of new spiritual music, gospel music, that is being composed. It is literally flooding the world. This reminds me of Isaiah 59:19 where it is written: When the enemy comes in like a flood, the Spirit of the Lord will lift up a standard against him. And this is precisely what is happening today on the music front. As a wave of satanic and godless music floods the market, the Lord is busy, through his children, to make music that is inspired by the Holy Spirit.

Psalm 22:3 reads as follows: *Yet you are holy, enthroned upon the praises of Israel.* By praise the Lord is exalted. God is surrounded by praise. A study of Revelation and the descriptions of heaven illustrate that the throne of God is surrounded day and night by praise and worship. When we read the Old Testament, we see the great variety of instruments that are used to praise God. An in-depth study of this topic brings us to the inevitable conclusion that song and music were an important part of temple life and also of the everyday lives of believers in the Old Testament.

Time and time again I have witnessed the power of song in situations where people were possessed. It sometimes happens that the demons in a person are very resistant. Often in such situations we start to praise God with songs of praise and sing about the blood of Christ. The effect is remarkable and the breakthrough often follows almost immediately.

I am convinced that spiritual music and song with praise and worship as theme will be of the utmost importance in years to come in the advancement of the gospel. It is also interesting to note how much music is currently released with praise and worship as theme. The Spirit of God is busy focusing our attention on something important. It is clear that praise and worship form part of the worldwide spiritual renewal in the church of Christ.

The place of spiritual music in prayer warfare cannot be underestimated. Think of David who played the harp for Saul. When he did this, the evil spirit left Saul and he came to his senses. Many women who have rebellious children and unsaved husbands tell of the calming effect on the whole family when spiritual music is played in the house.

Travail

In this chapter I make liberal use of information given in *Intercessory Prayer*, by Dutch Sheets and *Possessing the Gates of the Enemy,* by Cindy Jacobs.

What is travail?

The Lord here uses a physical phenomenon to explain a spiritual matter. In Galatians 4:19 Paul uses the Greek word *odino,* which has the meaning of a woman busy giving birth. Paul writes: *"... I am again in the pains of childbirth until Christ is formed in you ..."* Women who have children, and husbands who go through the whole birth process with them, know that birth is accompanied by pain. Women who have gone through it, know that giving birth involves your entire being. Paul says that he is in the pains of childbirth spiritually until Christ is formed in young believers. There are times in prayer that we are so occupied by the matter we are praying for that God, through his Spirit, lays such a burden on us, that it can be compared to someone giving birth. The woman in labour can think of nothing else but the child that has to be born from her body. There is no time for rest, to read the paper, watch TV or for joking. There is just one thing: the child must be born.

People who have been involved in intensive intercession for years can more or less all testify to personal experiences of spiritual labour pain. There are times that the matter you are praying for, rests so heavily on you that there is time for nothing else. You pray and pray until there is a breakthrough in the spiritual sphere. Only then you are able to rest and carry on with your normal tasks.

This type of prayer is not something you can generate by yourself. It is something that happens to you, the Holy Spirit brings it on you. Sometimes it takes a few hours or even days, at other times it only lasts a short while. It sometimes happens when a great number of people are praying for a matter. The Spirit of God often uses an individual, one of the last people to pray, to "give birth" to the answer. These kinds of prayers are often not as much words as sighs or groans to God. This is almost like Romans 8:26, namely that the Spirit of God intercedes for us with groans that words cannot express.

In travail there are often tears, groaning, pleading and loud cries to God. However, these outward signs are not always present. It could just be a very intense time of prayer. Travail can take place when a person is washing the car, mowing the lawn, doing shopping, etcetera. Travail is more common with intercessors than most people might think. But then again it happens that a person sometimes cries and screams in prayer and it has nothing to do with travail. Travail is not determined by visible behaviour, but by what happens in the spiritual sphere.

In the following paragraphs I will attempt to describe it. It is important that we take note of it so that we know what is happening to us or someone else when travail takes place.

Scriptures that bear relation to travail

In Galatians 4:19 Paul writes: *"My dear children, for whom I am again in the pains of childbirth until Christ is formed in you."*

In 1 Kings 18:41-45 we have the story of Elijah who prayed to God after three years and six months, to give rain again. The prayer position that Elijah takes, with his head between his knees, was the typical position of women of the time giving birth. Elijah was in travailing prayer. In James 5:16-17 it is referred to as "earnest/heartfelt" prayer. 1 Kings 18: 41-45: *And Elijah said to Ahab, "Go, eat and drink, for there is the sound of a heavy rain." ... Elijah climbed to the top of Carmel, bent down to the ground and put his face between his knees. "Go and look towards the sea," he told his servant. And he went up and looked. "There is nothing there," he said. Seven times Elijah said, "Go back." The seventh time the servant reported, "A cloud as small as a man's hand is rising from the sea." Meanwhile, the sky grew black with clouds ... a heavy rain came on ...*

Psalm 126 is a song in which a prayer is sung for the Lord to bring back the captives to Zion. Especially verses 5-6 contain an element which is indicative of travail: *Those who sow in tears will reap with songs of joy. He who goes out weeping, carrying seed to sow, will return with songs of joy, carrying sheaves with him.*

Isaiah 66:7-8: *"Before she goes into labour, she gives birth; before the pains come upon her, she delivers a son. Who has ever heard of such a thing? Who has ever seen such things? Can a country be born in a day or a nation be brought forth in a moment? Yet no sooner is Zion in labour than she gives birth to her children."*

The context of Romans 8:22-27 makes it clear that it is a reference to travail. We read in verse 22 that the whole creation is groaning as in the pains of childbirth. We read in verse 23 that we who have received the Spirit of God groan inwardly (in the pains of childbirth). In verses 26-27 we read: *In the same way, the Spirit helps us in our weakness. We do not know what we ought to pray for, but the Spirit himself intercedes for us with groans that words cannot express. And he who searches our hearts knows the mind of the Spirit, because the Spirit intercedes for the saints in accordance with God's will.*

In Matthew 26:36-39 we read about Jesus in Gethsemane. All the elements of travail are present in his prayer. He took Peter along with Him and the two sons of Zebedee: ... *and he began to be sorrowful and troubled. Then he said to them, "My soul is overwhelmed with sorrow to the point of death. Stay here and keep watch with me." Going a little farther, he fell with his face to the ground and prayed, "My Father, if it is possible, may this cup be taken from me."* In Luke 22:43-44 the veil is lifted a little more and we learn something more about what Matthew wrote when he said Jesus was in great anguish, to the point of death: *An angel from heaven appeared to him and strengthened him. And being in anguish, he prayed more earnestly, and his sweat was like drops of blood falling on the ground.*

Hebrews 5:7 teaches us more about *how* Jesus prayed and I believe that this verse reflects the essence of travail: *During the days of Jesus' life on earth, he offered up prayers and petitions with loud cries and tears to the one who could save him from death, and he was heard because of his reverent submission* [to God].

Bringing forth life

We read in John 7:38: *"...streams of living water will flow from within him."* The word "within" is the Greek word *koilia,* which means abdomen. In verse 39 it says: *By this he meant the Spirit, whom those who believed in him were later to receive.*

The Holy Spirit wants to use us, the spirit of the human being, as a womb to bring forth life. We cannot conceive this life, but we can release it. The Holy Spirit conceives life, but we, the believers, the intercessors, are the channels through which this new life is released.

It is difficult to explain precisely what travail is, but there are a few things to be said about it (cf. *Intercessory Prayer,* by Dutch Sheets):

- The Holy Spirit is involved.
- It is concerned with spiritual reproduction – the rebirth and conversion of the unsaved.
- It is concerned with prayer that is related to the spiritual maturity of believers.
- It can often be very intense prayer with outward manifestations like tears, fervency, loud exclamations and sighing (or groaning).
- It can sometimes result in signs and wonders that lead to the advancement of the kingdom.

The place of the Holy Spirit in travail

In travail the workings of the Holy Spirit are indispensable. The Holy Spirit is God's "birth agent" in the Holy Trinity. The Holy Spirit gives birth to spiritual life. In John 3:3-8 Jesus says: *"... no-one can see the kingdom of God unless he is born again ... no-one can enter the kingdom of God unless ... he is born of ... the Spirit. So it is with everyone born of the Spirit."* Only through the Holy Spirit can we be born again. It cannot be done by people. We read in Luke 1:35: *"The Holy Spirit will come upon you, and the power of the Most High will overshadow you."* Here again the Holy Spirit brings forth life. It concerns the birth of Jesus here, but it is still new life and in Jesus' case it was life that would lead to the redemption of humankind. The word "overshadow" is the Greek word *episkiazo.* Thyer, in his *Greek-English Lexicon of the New Testament,* describes the word as follows: "The Holy Spirit exerting creative energy upon the womb of the virgin Mary and impregnating it."

The Holy Spirit is the source of power in the Holy Trinity. Acts 1:8 teaches us that we will receive power when the Holy Spirit comes over us. In Luke 4:14 and 18 we read that Jesus came back, filled with the power of the Holy Spirit and because the Holy Spirit anointed Him, He could preach the gospel in all its fullness. The Holy Spirit was the power behind creation (Gen 1). He gives birth to the will of God. He blows the breath of life into the children of God and gives physical and spiritual life (Gen 2:7; Acts 2:1-4; Ezek 36:26-27; 37:9, 10, 14).

Elijah could not bring rain on Mount Carmel, but in James 5:16-19 we read that his prayers to God brought forth rain. Paul could not bring forth mature believers, but his prayers resulted in people growing to mature believers in Christ. The 120 people in the upstairs room did not have the power to start a church and maintain it, but by means of joint and prevailing prayer the Holy Spirit came upon them and something new came into being. It is clear that in each of these cases it was the Holy Spirit who brought it forth and effected it.

There is an inseparable connection between prayer and the Holy Spirit. Thus we can speak of prayer that gives birth.

In Genesis 1:2 it is written: *Now the earth was formless and empty, darkness was over the surface of the deep, and the Spirit of God was hovering over the waters.* The word "empty" is the Hebrew word *tohu,* which means "a desert, wild and empty, it lies useless, lifeless mass, formless." The basic meaning is that it is without life, without order, and sterile. The expression that the Spirit of God hovered over the waters is from the Hebrew word *rachap,* which literally means "to brood over". The use of this term in the description of creation links the Holy Spirit with the birth process or with bringing forth life. One dictionary defines *rachapo* as "brooding or fertilising." The word *rachap* is also sometimes used for the act of intercourse between a man and a woman whereby children are conceived. In John 1:1-3 and Colossians 1:16 we read that the Word created everything, but it was the Holy Spirit who brooded over the earth, who brought forth life, who gave birth to what Jesus spoke.

In Psalm 90:2 creation is compared to birth: *Before the mountains were born or you brought forth the earth and the world ...* The two words "born" and "brought forth" are the Hebrew words *yalad* and *chuwl.* Both words mean "to give birth". In Isaiah 66:8 we read: *Yet no sooner is Zion in labor (chuwl) than she gives birth (yalad) to her children.* By means of labour pains the Spirit of God wants to give birth to spiritual children (not only for Zion). Through the prayers of God's children, the Spirit of God wants to "brood over" people and bring about rebirth for them. But this process of spiritual birth occurs as a result of the Holy Spirit and the prayers (travailing intercession) of intercessors working together.

Dutch Sheets defines travail as follows: "A form of intercession that releases the creative power or energy of the Holy Spirit into a situation to produce, create or give birth to something."

When Elijah prayed on Mount Carmel, it produced rain. When Paul prayed in Galatians 4:19, his prayers produced mature believers. When the church prays according to Matthew 9:38, it can bring forth workers for the harvest. The prayers of the 120 that prayed for ten days in the upstairs room brought forth the outpouring of the Holy Spirit. When Hudson Taylor walked on the beach during the previous century and prayed, the *China Inland Mission* came into being. He kept on praying and God gave him 18 workers to go to China with him. In the ensuing years God sent out more than 1 000 workers in answer to travail.

An analogy of travail

The Holy Spirit wishes to release his creative life-giving power. The Spirit wants our cooperation in releasing his life-giving power in lifeless, fruitless, barren and humanly impossible situations. And this happens through prayer, intercessory prayer which in the end, results in travail.

We can pray for days, weeks, sometimes for months or years for a particular matter, until one day we are suddenly so burdened with this matter that we start praying intensely about it until there is a breakthrough. This period of intensive prayer is travailing prayer. It is especially during these periods (sometimes a few hours or a few days) that people plead with God with tears, supplication, groanings and sometimes loud cries.

It is very much like a pregnant woman. She carries the child in her for nine months. And then one morning, at a quarter past two, she wakes up. She feels the pains in her lower back and she knows: it is time for the baby to be born. As of that moment nothing matters to that woman but the fact that she is in labour and must give birth.

This is what happens to intercessors. They become "pregnant" by the Holy Spirit with a specific prayer assignment. It might be that the intercessor must pray for an unsaved person, or for a desperate situation in the church or someone in great need. The intercessor starts praying: for days, weeks, months and even years this matter/person is on the heart of the intercessor. But one day, when it is full-time, when the time for the spiritual rebirth has come, the Spirit of God comes over this person in extraordinary power and travail begins. And this lasts until the birth has taken place – until the person is saved, the matter resolved, there has been relief for the needy.

Spiritual abortions

Our age is the age of "legal" abortions. By legislation it is permissible in many countries to murder unborn babies. Since February 1997 it is legal in South Africa to have an abortion done. By the end of 1997, 20 000 women in South Africa had already had abortions. Many Christians are upset by abortions, and rightly so. But I am worried about the hundreds of thousands of spiritual abortions that take place almost daily. What do I mean by spiritual abortions? Spiritual abortions take place when the Holy Spirit gives a prayer burden to an intercessor/ Christian, but that person does not respond. Sometimes a person reacts to the promptings of the Holy Spirit and starts praying for a specific unsaved person or matter, but when a few days or weeks have passed, the intercessor stops praying. The effect is the same as that of a woman who has an abortion done. The prayer assignment is not completed, the intercessor does not keep on praying until the spiritual birth has taken place.

This is a serious matter. The problem does not lie with the Holy Spirit who calls upon us to pray. The problem lies with Christians who do not pray or do not persist in prayer until the answer comes, the matter has been prayed through or the spiritual birth has taken place.

15

Intercession as supplication

Intercession has supplication at its core; that is to plead with God. Supplication is an integral aspect of intercession. The intercessor is someone who pleads. He pleads with God to have mercy. How difficult modern man finds it to plead and to petition. In some spiritual circles supplication is associated with people who have not grown much spiritually. How tragic that some believers can become so "big", so mature that they are above pleading with God.

Supplication is a term that is used often in the Scriptures in connection with prayer and intercession. Supplication and travail are very closely related. According to *Strong's Concordance,* supplication contains a strong element of begging. It is to plead and beg with God. To beseech and ask urgently and intensely. We, for example, read in Acts 1:14 that the disciples were joined together in prayer, that they devoted themselves steadfastly to prayer and supplication. Philippians 4:6 says that we should make our requests known to God by prayer and *petition/supplication.* 1 Timothy 2:1-2 says that we should pray for all people with supplication, prayers, intercessions and thanksgiving, for kings and those in authority so that we may lead a quiet and peaceful life.

Moses pleaded with God for the people of Israel. He called upon God during the ten plagues over Egypt. He lay prostrate before God, for forty days and nights and pleaded for mercy. Abraham petitioned before God for Sodom and Gomorrah.

Hebrews 5:7 teaches us that Jesus pleaded with his Father with prayers and petitions, with loud cries and tears. Think about it: if the Son of God pleaded and petitioned before his Father, how much more should we not do it as broken, sinful people?

Is it not Paul who, after a lifetime of spiritual work, writes from prison to the believers in Philippi: *The Lord is near ... in everything, by prayer and petitions, with thanksgiving, present your requests to God* (Phil 4:5-6). Paul, mature in the faith, encourages believers to come to God with supplication.

Hannah, in 1 Samuel 1-2 is an excellent example of someone who knew the word supplication. Hannah was mocked and scorned by Elkanah's other wife, Peninnah, because she didn't have children. Hannah saw only one way out; she had to go to the Lord and pray for a child of her own. She went to the temple. She knew exactly what she wanted: a boy. No, a daughter would not do, it would not take her shame away. In the temple Hannah prayed, she pleaded. She did not eat (she fasted). She poured out her soul before the Lord, she cried before Him. She did not try to be dignified. She did not try to project the correct image or to pray "well". She did not care what people thought. Eventually Eli arrived and thought she was drunk. People didn't understand her, but God did. He heard her prayer and supplication and He answered her. At a certain point Hannah realised that she had had a breakthrough and that

God had heard her supplication.

The story in Luke 18:1-8, where Jesus tells of the persistent widow who went to the unjust judge day after day and pleaded with him to grant her justice, is an example of supplication. Supplication has an element of unceasing prayer. Matthew 7:7 teaches us to keep on praying, knocking, seeking. This is the attitude of a person who pleads.

Believers who prayed for revival through the ages, understood the secret of supplication. They were so desperate that they did not mind pleading.

Those who plead have learnt the secret that there is nothing good in them. Nothing in ourselves makes us worthy enough to ask God to do something for us. Only the person who truly realises his or her own spiritual bankruptcy before God and understands that everything is from and through and to God, can plead. Whoever pleads, does not lay claim to merit, but to grace. Oh, and how we need grace. Grace and mercy. John 1:16 teaches us that out of the fullness of his grace we receive one blessing after another.

Supplication and tears

Supplication and travail are often accompanied by tears. Crying during intercession is quite common. A missionary was part of a prayer team in Damaraland (in the Northwest of Namibia) and as they were praying for the Damara people, he had a remarkable experience. After they had been praying for a day or two, one of the ladies in the team started crying. She cried almost all day. Afterwards she said she had no control over it. She had started crying about the sins and brokenness of the Damara people. It was as if God was revealing through this outward sign how He felt about these people and their sin. It was quite clearly the work of the Holy Spirit and not something she herself would choose to do. When you are at the disposal of the Holy Spirit, He uses it as a form of prayer to achieve his specific goal. There are similar incidents of intercession from other parts of the world.

Intercessors as beggars

Charles Spurgeon compares supplication with a beggar asking for bread. In his plea for bread a beggar will always have a good argument as to why you should give him money or bread. To one man he will say, "Sir, we know each other, you know I have nothing, give me a piece of bread. I know you care about me." He will say to another, "Sir, we will see each other only this once; help me with a piece of bread." The one who begs has no shame, he is driven by his need. He cannot afford pride. And it is precisely this that makes his plea so precious to God. God resists the haughty, but He has mercy on the humble.

Beggars are unashamed, like the unashamed friends in Luke 11:5-11. They beg, plead and implore because their lives depend on it. If they are too proud to beg, they will die of hunger. They have lost all their shame, embarrassment, pride and all haughtiness. There is no such thing as a conceited beggar. They cannot afford it.

God is looking for people who come to Him unashamedly, who pray without pride and arrogance.

Before the National Day of Prayer on 7 July 1996 a friend and I worked together on a pamphlet in which we wanted to give information and prayer directives and hand out to people on the National Day of Prayer.

We presented the pamphlet to a couple of spiritual leaders for their comment before we printed it. In one place we used the following words: "Plead with God that in his grace, He will give revival." One of the leaders crossed out the word "plead" and explained that the church group he belonged to did not like the word "plead". It is too negative and doesn't make a good impression. He suggested that at most, we use the word "ask".

Friends, this is pride and does not indicate brokenness. When we have become spiritually mature to the extent that we cannot plead anymore and beg God to help us, then we are *too* mature.

Intercession is wrestling with God

Intercession is to wrestle with God

In prayer, wrestling has two facets. One part involves the Evil One, but the second facet of wrestling is to wrestle with God. In this chapter I would like to concentrate only on the aspect of wrestling with God.

The intercessor wrestles *with* God and *together with* God. In Genesis 32 Jacob wrestles with God. In Genesis 32:28 we read one of the most extraordinary remarks in the entire Bible: *"Your name will no longer be Jacob, but Israel, because you have struggled with God and with men and have overcome."* Take note that the word Israel literally means to wrestle with God. The "person" with whom Jacob wrestled that night at the Jabbok River was most probably God Himself. This can be deduced from the name "Israel". Verse 28 says that Jacob had overcome God and men. Think about this for a moment: Jacob overcame God! Could this be possible? Yes, the Bible says so very clearly. Jacob overcame God because God wanted to be overcome by Jacob. God took the first step; He came to Jacob during the night, there at the Jabbok, and started wrestling with him. Of course God was stronger than Jacob, but God allowed Jacob to overcome Him. Jacob's intercession saved his life, but also that of his descendants from the hand and wrath of Esau, and from his descendants the people of Israel were born.

In Luke 22:44 we read how Jesus wrestles with his Father in Gethsemane. When we read in Hebrews 5:7: *During the days of Jesus' life on earth, he offered up prayers and petitions with loud cries and tears,* it means that Jesus wrestled more than once with his Father. Jesus' struggle in Gethsemane was exceptional. His sweat was mixed with blood, blood that was dripping from his forehead because of the struggle.

In Colossians 4:12-13 we read that Epaphras steadfastly and earnestly prayed for the believers in Colosse. But it was not ordinary prayer. The words to "wrestle in prayer", used in Colossians 4:12, is the Greek word *agonizomat,* which means to struggle, to agonize, to wrestle, to fight, to strive.

When Moses prayed for the people on the mountain in Exodus 32, and when Elijah prayed for rain in 1 Kings 18, both of them wrestled with God. There was no suggestion at all of a struggle with Evil. The struggle was with God. When God seeks someone in Ezekiel 22:30 to stand before Him in the gap for the city, He is in fact looking for someone to wrestle with Him for the survival of the city. When Isaiah 62:6-7 calls upon us to remind God day and night of his promises, it contains an element of struggle.

When Jesus teaches the disciples in Luke 18:1-8 to pray steadfastly and not give up, he also refers to the widow who went to the judge *every day* and pleaded with him to grant her justice. Here we also become aware of the concept of struggle. To the widow it was a spiritual struggle. Thus Jesus wants to draw our attention to the fact that prayer is a spiritual struggle.

"Let me go!"

When Jacob wrestles with God that night, God says, "Let me go!" But Jacob goes on wrestling. It is as if God cannot go while Jacob refuses to let Him go. God bound Himself by means of his promises to listen to us.

Moses wrestles with God on the mountain to save Israel. God says to Moses, "Leave me alone!" We get the impression that God cannot leave unless Moses decides to let Him go.

Of course God is almighty and God can push Moses away. But God binds Himself by his promises and his character to listen to a man or woman who grabs hold of Him in prayer, who wrestles with Him, who acts as intercessor (Isa. 64:7). This is why God changes his mind when Jeremiah goes on pleading for deliverance, when Amos wrestles with God not to destroy the people (Amos 7), when Elijah is on the mountain and sends his servant back seven times to check if there are any clouds, when Hannah comes to God with prayer and supplication to plead for a son, when Moses pleads with God in Numbers 14 not to reject the people of Israel when they do not trust the Lord to drive away the enemy from them, and in this way underestimate God. This is why God takes 21 days to answer Daniel and why God comes to meet and fortify his Son in Gethsemane. This is why the Lord Jesus allows the disciples in John 6 to carry on working with Him.

The secret was someone who caught hold of God and said, "I will not let You go!"

17

Prevailing

intercession

Pray and do not give up

In the Bible Jesus teaches us to persist in prayer; to pray and not give up (Luke 18:1). In 1 Thessalonians 5:18 Paul calls upon us to pray continually. All through the Scriptures there is strong emphasis on prevailing prayer. Sometimes the term *praying through* is used and this also includes travail, which is discussed previously.

The Bible teaches us very distinctly that we should pray continually and not give up. The expression "continual/constant" (Greek: *ektenes* and *adialeiptos)* is used only six times in the New Testament and every time it is connected to prayer. It is as if God wants to make sure that is the one thing we will not give up on, but do continually:

- ...but *constant* (happening all the time/without stopping) prayer was offered to God for him ... (Acts 12:5; NKJV).

- … I remember you in my prayers *at all times* (without stopping/incessantly) … (Rom 1:9).
- We *continually* (without stopping) remember before our God and Father your work produced by faith … (1 Thess 1:2-3).
- And we also thank God *continually* (without stopping) … (1 Thess 2:13).
- Pray *continually* (without stopping) (1 Thess 5:17).
- … I *constantly* (without stopping) remember you in my prayers (2 Tim 1:3).

Jesus taught his disciples that "they should always pray and not give up" (Luke 18:1). In Matthew 7:7 where Jesus taught his disciples the principles of the kingdom, He said, "Ask and it will be given to you …" The Greek literally says, "Pray continually (all the time/without stopping) and it will be given to you continually (all the time)." There is however, more in the Bible about prevailing prayer.

The Greek word *proskartereo* (persistently/continually) is translated in *Strong's Greek Dictionary* as follows: "keep at it, persevere, be a stayer, show stamina, stick at it, keep awake, to be earnest towards, be constantly diligent."

- "Continue earnestly in prayer" (Col 4:2; NKJV).
- "… continuing steadfastly in prayer" (Rom 12:12; NKJV).
- "But we will give ourselves continually to prayer and the ministry of the word" (Acts 6:4; NKJV).
- "Praying always with all prayer and supplication in the Spirit, being watchful to this end with all perseverance …" (Eph 6:18; NKJV).

Prayer may never be anything but persistent, continual prayer. Prayer expects an answer and only when the answer has been given, that prayer is concluded. Prayer without an answer is a contradiction; it is impossible. The Bible declares emphatically that prayer will be answered: *For everyone who asks receives; he who seeks finds; and to him who knocks, the door will be opened"* (Matt 7:8), and: *This is the confidence we have in approaching God: that if we ask anything according to his will, he hears us. And if we know that he hears us – whatever we ask – we know that we have what we asked of him* (1 John 5:14-15).

They persevered

Hannah persisted in prayer until she was given an answer. In 1 Samuel we read how Hannah poured out her heart in prayer, stopped eating for a day and was in tears before the Lord. And then finally, in Samuel 1:18 we read: *Then she went her way and ate something, and her face was no longer downcast.* What is the meaning of this? Hannah knew she had received an answer – she prayed through. Towards the end of the year Hannah became pregnant and gave birth to a son.

Moses lay prostrate before God for 40 days and 40 nights and prayed. He persisted in prayer until he gained God's mercy and help for the people of Israel (Deut 9:25-29).

Elijah prayed for the people of Israel for three years and six months to leave Baal and return to the Lord God (1 Kings 17-18). He persisted in prayer until the Lord answered with fire from heaven. Then he prayed for rain. Seven times he sent his servant to see if there was any sign of rain and then, at last, his servant reported: There is a cloud as big as a man's hand!

Daniel prayed for 21 days before an angel of the Lord came with a message (Dan 10:2-21). Day after day he persisted in prayer. He did not say at the end of the third day, "Oh well, the Lord will probably do what He wishes at a later stage." No, for 21 days he ate dry bread and drank water. He fasted and prayed. He knew God was alive, that God answered prayer. In the past God answered him and there was no reason why God wouldn't do it again now. On the 21st day the angel came. And what a revelation the angel brought about a mighty battle he was involved in with the prince of Persia. The answer to prayer was delayed by this war in the heavens, but I am sure the angel was also encouraged to carry on fighting every time he looked down to earth and saw Daniel on his knees, waiting for an answer that the angel of the Lord had to bring him. Daniel prayed continually until there was a breakthrough, until the answer came.

Pray until you get your answer – this is prayer. The essence of prayer lies in God who answers prayer. Talking to God is meaningless if there are no answers to prayer.

Praying through

One of the secrets of intercession is *praying through*. Unfortunately many intercessors find this principle strange. We grew up in an atmosphere where the practice of praying through was not part of the normal prayer life of the church of Christ. I must admit that in my own life, it was only in recent years that the Lord made me aware of this facet through his Holy Spirit. I have attended many prayer meetings and spent many hours in prayer. But it is something else to pray and to carry on praying *until* there is a breakthrough in the spiritual realm. Often people pray for hours, and week after week they pray for the same matters, but it is as if the matter or matters are never settled spiritually.

For example, we pray for revival, but we don't get the feeling that we are progressing. We pray for marriages, the salvation of Moslems or Hindus, more missionaries in the field, a change in the finances of our church, etcetera. But there seems to be no progress. We pray for the workings of God's Spirit during worship services and that the congregation will attend church again to hear the Word, but it seems as if nothing is happening.

Take a look at Daniel in Daniel 10. He started praying and 21 days later he was still on his knees. Why? He prayed and waited for an answer. The answer, the breakthrough only came after 21 days of continual prayer and partial fasting. However, he persisted in this one matter until the answer came. Unaware of the battle in which Gabriel, who was on the way with the answer was involved in and subsequently detained, he persisted in prayer until Gabriel broke through to bring the answer. We read how Elijah prayed on Mount Carmel – hour after hour he prayed. Time and time again he sent his servant to see if there were some clouds in the sky. The seventh time the servant came back with the news that he could see a cloud as big as a man's hand – this was the breakthrough. Think of the church in Acts 12 that was praying for Peter in prison. They prayed through the night – until the angel woke Peter and God opened the prison gates for him. The apostles sat in the upper room for ten days. They persevered, steadfastly united in prayer and on the tenth day God poured his Spirit out on the church. The promise of Jesus in Acts 1:8 and Luke 24:49 is kept. They *prayed through.* Paul and Silas were in prison in Acts 16, they prayed and sang songs of praise to God – suddenly the breakthrough came. There was an earthquake and God turned the impossible situation around. The jailer was saved and Paul and Silas were freed from jail.

I cannot emphasise enough that we must make more of the principle of *praying through.* It is not enough to merely pray. We must look to God for the answers. Why is there no breakthrough, no answer to prayer? What hinders an answer from coming through? So often we pray and just ask that the Lord will answer, but too often it happens that we do not ask the Lord what it is that is holding back the answers to our prayers.

Recently I was with a group of fifty people before the throne of God in a time of prayer where we prayed for a spiritual breakthrough in a specific congregation. We started praying and asked the Lord to give revival in this church and to make the church a home of prayer for the nations. After an hour and a half I felt that we weren't making any progress. Something was hindering our prayers. We asked the Lord to show us what it was. Little by little, the Holy Spirit pointed out different sins to the small prayer groups as they prayed. Some sins concerned things that happened in the past of that church and other were sins present in the lives of those who prayed. Those sins were confessed before the Lord one by one. And then the breakthrough came. Without anybody having to say it, we all knew that God had heard us and that we had prayed through. Our hearts were filled with joy and gladness. We knew our work was finished for now and we could go to bed. We had started praying that evening at 22:30 and by 01:30 the following morning we knew that we had prayed through and that God had answered. The next morning in the worship service God was powerfully at work in the congregation – it was in answer to the prayers of the previous night.

Two words describe this matter of praying through very well: the words *prevailing prayer* and *travail*. The first, prevailing prayer is the persistent prayer that Luke talks about, for example in Luke 18:1-8. In this passage he calls upon the disciples to pray all the time and not give up or lose heart. He uses the example of a persistent widow who kept on going to a callous, hard-hearted judge, day after day, to plead that he grant her justice against her adversary – she did this until he helped her. By this Jesus does not want to say God the Father is like that judge; on the contrary, God wants to help us and He will help us. Jesus goes one step further and says that God will help us *quickly*. 1 Thessalonians 5:17 confirms that we should pray continually/without ceasing, that we must persist in prayer until the answer comes.

Travail is another important aspect of persistent prayer and of praying through. This aspect has been discussed and here I simply refer to it in passing. The word travail has the meaning of giving birth, being in labour. Giving birth is often an immensely intense and painful process. When a woman gives birth, her total being is caught up in this one matter: "The child that is inside my body must be born." Her entire being is involved in this process. This is the case with intercessors also. They will pray for months and years, but one day God will "grab" them and spiritually they go into labour, as in childbirth. Through prayer they will give birth to a matter that they are praying for. It is often accompanied by tears, pleading, supplication and extended hours of prayer until a breakthrough comes. Sometimes it takes a few hours, sometimes days.

What we need today is intercessors who can persist in prayer and who are available to be used by the Spirit of God to spiritually, by means of intercession, give birth to the new things God wishes to do in our times. As we move closer to the times of the new things that God wants to do, the prayer burden will become heavier and the times of prayer more intense. There will be fewer words to express the things God wants from us. It will turn into a groaning. Take a look at Romans 8:26 – the Spirit of God will intercede for us with groans that words cannot express. Isaiah 53:11 describes how Jesus was in travail for us. It absorbed his entire being and cost Him his life, but it brought salvation for humankind.

Signs of breakthrough

People often ask how long we should pray before it is enough. In other words, how do we know when to stop praying for something? There are several ways in which we can tell when prayer has been answered.

a) When I am not reminded continuously by the Spirit to pray for a matter, I know the matter has been settled. Put in another way: the prayer burden will disappear when God has answered.
b) When there is no desire anymore to pray for the matter. In

other words, there is no unction from the Holy Spirit to pray. This might be an indication that the matter has been concluded.

c) When the Holy Spirit starts guiding me to scriptures that indicate that the victory has been gained.
d) When we can tell from the circumstances that the matter is settled and that further prayer is not necessary – for example if the person who has been prayed for is healed, or if the prayer was for a person to become converted and he/she has repented and renounced sin.

How often it happens that we start praying for a matter and give up later because we lose hope and are not sensitive to the guidance of the Holy Spirit? This is a strategy that the devil uses to make us despondent before the breakthrough comes. Daniel was in a spiritual position of intercession before God for twenty-one days. What would the outcome have been if Daniel got up after ten or fifteen days and carried on with his job as politician? The angel would have come and Daniel would not have been ready to receive God's answer. I suspect that God might even have called the angel back. Is it possible that the angel would not have been able to break through the opposition of the prince of Greece if Daniel did not persist in prayer? I don't know. What I do know is that prayer releases power and that God in his sovereignty decided to respond to prayer. I also know that there comes a point where a matter has been prayed through. Until we reach that point, there is no breakthrough.

It might be that the Lord gives us the conviction that a matter has been concluded, settled without us seeing a visible breakthrough. The following anecdote is a good example of this. At Lausanne II a group of intercessors prayed for a missionary by the name of Bruce Olson. At that stage he had been the prisoner of a group of terrorists for more than nine months who wanted to use him as a kind of hostage to a certain Indian tribe, and they also threatened to kill him. The intercession team

experienced very clearly at one stage that there had been a breakthrough and that Bruce Olson would be set free. Thus they stopped praying. Bruce Olson was set free a week later. Thus the matter can be settled in the spiritual sphere, while the outward circumstances still seem unchanged.

Intercession and fasting

Fasting in the Scriptures

Fasting is not unfamiliar to the Old or New Testament. Moses, Elijah, Ezekiel, Samuel, Daniel, Ezra, John the Baptist, the disciples, Jesus, Paul and many prominent persons in the Bible fasted and prayed.

Jesus did not revoke the practice of fasting when He came; on the contrary, He came to confirm it. He began his public ministry with a 40-day fast. In Matthew 6:16-18 Jesus gives directives for when someone fasts. He says quite clearly: ***"When you fast …"*** Nowhere in the New Testament is fasting revoked. According to his own testimony, Paul also fasted often. It is simply not true that fasting is an Old Testament practice that does not feature in the New Testament. I also often hear the argument that fasting is not "Reformed"/Calvanistic. It is not true. The Reformers, the people who put the Calvanistic doctrine into words, were people who were in deadly earnest about fasting and praying and also wrote about it. Over the past four ages practically all the main church traditions have been serious about fasting and praying: Anglican, Methodist, Presbyterian, Puritan, Wesleyan, Charismatic and Pentecostal groups, Reformed, Baptist etc.

Fasting as practice in the church through the ages

We learn from a document of the early Christian church, the *Didache,* that these Christians prayed and fasted every Wednesday and Friday. The Reformers were men who were familiar with fasting and praying. Martin Luther was a man who often sought the Lord's face in fasting and prayer. John Calvin fasted and prayed until the greater part of Geneva became converted to God. In Calvin's writings he pays a lot of attention to fasting. John Knox fasted and prayed and the godless queen, Mary, Queen of Scotland, Bloody Mary, said she feared no armed force in the world as much as she feared the prayers of John Knox. In his lifetime John Knox fasted and prayed and pleaded with God for Scotland with the words, "Lord, give me Scotland or I die!" And in his lifetime Knox saw and experienced a movement in which almost the whole of Scotland turned to God.

We have examples of prominent leaders over the past 300 years who fasted and prayed. Jonathan Edwards, the brilliant American theologian and God's instrument in the revival of the eighteenth century in the USA, often fasted and prayed. David Brainerd, the well-known missionary to the American Indians, was a man who had intense periods of fasting and praying and saw great breakthroughs among the Indians. John Wesley fasted twice a week and all the Methodist preachers of his time were in the habit of fasting weekly and often presided at prolonged times of fasting and praying. Charles Finney, one of the greatest evangelists and revivalist leaders in history, and a man who in his lifetime saw more than half a million people becoming converted, often withdrew to pray and fast in solitude.

Examples of fasting and prayer in our times

Many Christians still find the concept of fasting and prayer a strange one. For almost 100 years (approximately 1860-1960) not a single book was written on the topic of fasting and praying. Since the nineteen sixties this Biblical practice received some attention again. Initially it was only individuals, but later on prayer groups took up the matter again and currently we see that entire congregations, denominations and even large groupings of Christians on a national and international level are taking the matter of fasting and prayer seriously again.

In his very well-known book, *Celebration of Discipline,* Richard Forster has made a significant contribution towards bringing the concept of fasting to the attention of the broader ecclesiastical public. Books on fasting and prayer by other authors like David Smith (*Fasting)* and Arthur Wallace (*God's chosen fast)* have also contributed greatly. Today we hardly find a single book that takes prayer seriously in which fasting is not discussed as well.

Bill Bright's book, *The Coming Revival: A call to Fast, Pray and "Seek God's Face"* was inspired by his own experience of a 40-day fast. In this book he describes how the Lord called upon him to find two million Christians to pray for revival in the church. The book is busy impacting large parts of the body of Christ worldwide.

Since Bill Bright's book in 1995, up until the end of 1997,

there have already been numerous national and international initiatives where large groups of Christians fasted for 40 days and prayed for revival on a national and international level.

During 1994, before the first democratic elections in South Africa, there were two periods of 40 days in which Christians fasted. The first was from 2 January to 10 February 1994 and the second followed directly afterwards. I believe it was, amongst other things, these intense times of prayer that contributed towards the peaceful transition to multiparty democracy.

As from 29 May to 7 July 1996 approximately 100 000 Christians in South Africa took part in a 40-day fast where prayers were said for Christians to humble themselves about sin in the country and the sins of our forefathers. The theme of this time of prayer was *Healing the Land* and it was concluded with the national Day of Prayer on 7 July 1996 at the Union Buildings in Pretoria.

During 1997 a new phenomenon made its appearance. Individual congregations and even groups of congregations and churches started fasting and praying for 40 days. In Pretoria just a few churches took part. In Natal quite a good many churches fasted and prayed for revival. I know of approximately 10-12 initiatives at local churches that fasted and prayed for 40 days towards the end of 1997 for spiritual awakening or revival.

On an international level numerous similar drives were launched in the following three years. By the end of 1997 there was an initiative to involve hundreds of churches in Europe in 40 days of fasting and prayer. It was followed up immediately with a new 40-day fast early in 1998 for churches who had not been aware of it or whose programmes did not allow them to take part in November–December 1997. In England, the USA and many other countries, 40-day periods are blocked out for fasting and praying for revival.

In South Africa a 40-day period of fasting and praying was planned from 12 April to 21 May 1998 (from Resurrection Day to

Ascension Day) with the theme: *Prepare the way for the Lord.* More than 500 000 Christians over all language and church barriers were involved.

What is fasting and praying all about?

To fast means to place God first and to focus on God. There are times when we can carry on with our everyday lives, but then there are times that God calls us to set everything aside and to seek his face in fasting and praying and to intercede for specific matters.

I believe with all my heart that something which is done in response to a direct order from God should be done under his guidance. I am not a supporter myself of a regular fast one or two days a week. It could cause fasting to become routine and later legalism (it need not necessarily be the case). Every period of fasting must be initiated by God. The Lord could call upon us to fast and pray for a day, three days, or even one day per week for a specific period of time until there is a breakthrough.

Fasting also has the character of prevailing prayer. This means to be in earnest with God, to set all other things aside, also food, so that you can focus your full attention on God. Fasting is an effective way to get all hindrances out of the way so that you are able, with singleness of purpose, to give your full attention to the matter you are praying for.

Fasting is *not* a hunger-strike or a means to manipulate God. This is why it is important that fasting be initiated by God. God calls upon us to fast. No one really understands why it is necessary to fast, but God wants it. He decides and encourages his children to fast and pray in certain situations.

Sometimes fasting is a sign of atonement and of grief (Lev 23-27; Joel 2:12; Deut 9:25-29). At other times fasting can be a praise-offering to the Lord and it contains an element of joy and gladness (Ps 50:14 and 23; Zech 8:19). Sometimes fasting is of help in intercession and at other times we fast for personal requests, personal growth and victory over sin, or sometimes also in situations of particular pressure or onslaughts.

The attitude of the heart

Prayer must always come from a pure heart. And fasting too. God expects sincerity and obedience. These are the conditions for fasting.

Fasting is not done to perform a duty. Fasting comes from a heart that cares, a compassionate heart and a heart that is focused on God. Isaiah 58 gives a number of guidelines and directives for those who want to fast:

- We should humble ourselves before God and humiliate ourselves (v 5).
- Those who are in bondage unjustly must be set free (v 6).
- To set the oppressed free and break every yoke carried by people (v 6).
- To share your food with the hungry, provide a place to stay for the homeless, clothes for those who do not have any and not to abandon them to their fate (v 7).

Fasting is not something passive. It is not only to deny yourself food and to pray. No, it is also to actively heed the commands of God in Isaiah 58.

The person who is fasting, is not trying to earn God's blessings, because he/she is fasting on God's instruction. There is no mention of gain, but definitely of obedience. Fasting is not a substitute for obedience or confessing and renouncing your sin. Fasting does not replace the direct assignment from God to help the needy.

Those who fast are not trying to impress others with their "spirituality". Fasting is a matter between you and the Lord and the fewer the people who know about it, the better. Fasting is a spiritual act and not a physical occurrence. We must guard against fasting taking on an outward form.

Fasting may never be done in a legalistic manner. It may not become a new rule in your life, a yardstick that you use to measure your own life or the lives of other believers. In fasting it is not about how many days you fast, how little water you drink, or on what kind of fast you go. Fasting is concerned with the fact that the person who fasts focuses his whole being on God. I know of people who "fasted" by not watching TV for a week, and God used it powerfully in their lives. Let us not make rules for one another on how to fast. Fasting is a personal matter between you and the Lord.

The spiritual power of fasting

Fasting sets God's power free in times of need. In Joshua 7:6 we read how Joshua and the elders of Israel fasted and prayed and that God answered them. One of the results of this period of fasting and prayer was that Joshua and his army took the city of Ai. In Judges 20 we read how the people of Israel fought the Benjamites and lost time and time again. They fasted and prayed and God gave them the victory. In Ezra 8:21-23 we read how Ezra and the exiles had a day of fasting at the Ahava Canal where they asked God to protect them on the dangerous journey ahead. Verse 23 reads: "*So we fasted and petitioned our God about this, and he answered our prayer.*"

Joshua 7:6 also gives us an indication that fasting can be used to find out what is wrong. Israel lost against the small city of Ai after conquering the mighty Jericho. What went wrong? Joshua and the elders lay prostrate before God for a whole day and God answered them.

Prayer and fasting bring the Power of God into our lives.

Pastor Hsi, a well-known Chinese leader, was once in a very difficult situation. His wife had many problems and there were definite onslaughts from the Evil One. He withdrew into a room for three days where he fasted and prayed in solitude. After three days he came out of the room, filled with the power of the Lord, went up to his wife and prayed a simple prayer for her. She was instantaneously free and could carry on with her life in the normal way.

In history God often led Christians to fast and pray and this brought breakthroughs in their personal lives. Often Christians experienced that the Lord set them free from secret sins and gave them the victory over sin.

Prayer and fasting bring wisdom, revelation and guidance. Daniel fasted on bread and water for 21 days before an angel of the Lord brought him a message. The entire part in Exodus 19-31 is a revelation of God in answer to fasting and praying. Moses was in God's presence without food and water for 40 days while this revelation was given to him.

When we are involved in spiritual warfare, fasting plays a very important role. Prayer and fasting are two inseparable parts of the same thing. In 2 Chronicles 20:1-30 we read about the Moabites and Ammonites who came with a mighty army to make war against Judah. Jehoshaphat proclaimed a day of fasting and prayer for all the people and asked God to intervene. The Lord brought about a mighty and supernatural victory. It was the result of fasting and prayer.

Dick Eastman uses the term "fasting down of strongholds". Time and again we see in the Scriptures that praying together with fasting results in supernatural events. There is a spiritual power that accompanies fasting that cannot be rationally explained by the human mind. In Matthew 17:19-21 the disciples asked Jesus why the demon did not want to leave the child while they prayed for him. Jesus answered, *"Because you have so little faith ... But this kind does not go out except by prayer and fasting."* The faith that overcomes stubborn opposition, like resistance of evil spirits, is only possible for those who live in close communion with God and who withdraw from the world to pray and fast. Certain types of resistance and strongholds of the Evil One are only broken by means of fasting and prayer. It is through fasting that intercession often develops to the full. Fasting, intercession and prayer warfare are very closely linked. It was through fasting and prayer that Jesus triumphed over Satan's temptations in Matthew 4.

Many times in the past God gave revival in answer to intensive periods of fasting and prayer. Most of the hundreds of revivals over the past 300 years were preceded by people who, amongst other things, fasted and prayed.

Nations, countries and cities have been spared and saved when people have humbled themselves before God. Queen Esther called out a three day total fast and this saved the exiled people of Israel from extinction. Jonah proclaimed God's judgment over the city of Nineveh and the king and all the inhabitants of the city humbled themselves before God and put on sackcloth and for three days they made atonement with prayer and fasting. The whole city was spared.

There are thousands of examples of children of the Lord who went into solitude to fast and pray for friends or family to be saved. Time and time again the Lord answered them and extraordinary conversions and miracles took place.

19

Danger areas in Intercession

Wrong motives

1. Manipulation

There are many intercessors who try to manipulate God into answering their prayers. Such persons try all kinds of arguments with the Lord to get their way. God will not allow anyone to manipulate Him.

It also happens quite often that intercessors try to manipulate spiritual leaders with their prayers. It happens that intercessors have a certain idea of the direction that the church must move into, or they believe the minister or the pastor does not hear the Lord correctly. Then they start manipulating the minister or pastor to do what they want. Such intercessors normally find it difficult to handle authority. This attitude kills prayer. If the spiritual leader does not address the matter in his church and deal with it, it will mean the spiritual death of his church.

2. Haughtiness

Haughtiness poses one of the greatest dangers for intercessors. It happens only too often that God answers the prayers of intercessors and that the intercessors become secretly proud. Pride among intercessors takes on many forms. Some look down on the prayers of other believers who don't have the same "knowledge" that they have, or can also pray in tongues the way they do, or *cannot* pray in tongues! Others tell everybody who wants to listen about their wonderful answers to prayer under the pretext that they are bearing testimony to the greatness of God. But if you listen closely, it is merely pride and boastfulness under a thin veneer.

I don't know of a greater danger to intercessors than haughtiness. We so easily think we "know" how to do it and start behaving like experts. John Dawson, leader of the *Reconciliation Coalition* made the following remark on occasion: "There is no such thing as a black belt intercessor." Too often I hear of intercessors who believe they have reached spiritual levels and heights that others have not even heard of. Let us be careful.

The most important qualification of an intercessor is brokenness and humility.

3. A judgmental disposition and bitterness

A disposition of bitterness and a judgmental frame of mind turn the intercessor into a judge. Jesus did not come as a judge. With the Second Coming He will come as a judge, but with his first coming He came for the people, to intercede for them with God. This should be the attitude of the intercessor.

It often happens that we see sin and unrighteousness around us. It upsets us and when we pray, we are judgmental towards those who sin and are unrighteous. This is when we become judges instead of intercessors. Instead of praying for them, we accuse them before God. We use the words that are suitable to intercession, but in our hearts we judge.

God asks that we, like Christ, will be distressed and mournful about sin and will intercede for those who transgressed, so that He can be merciful.

4. Dictating to God

Many intercessors, under the impression that they are praying specifically, are in fact busy dictating to God how He should do his work. It is our job to pray and God's job to answer those prayers.

I sometimes find it amazing how presumptuous we can be at times. Just listen to your own prayers. We pray as if God is not aware of what is going on in his creation and as if He is mentally retarded and we need to help Him do his work by means of our prayers. God knows what to do. One of God's major frustrations is to get us and our good intentions out of the way so that He can get to work.

5. Own advantage

Too many of our prayers, no matter how holy they may sound, are at the deepest level filled with quite a few advantages for ourselves. We can pray very piously, but there are so many hidden motives.

For example, when we are being persecuted, we often pray that the Lord will protect his honour and that the persecution stops. Too often I have seen in my own life that my prayers in such times have precious little to do with the honour of God. They are concerned much more with my "good name". And let's be honest: often when people gossip about us or backbite or slander us, they don't even know half of the things we did. In fact, most of us are actually being flattered by the remarks vindictive people make about us. We are in fact far worse than they make us out to be.

James 4:2-3 clearly says that we pray and do not receive, because our prayers are focused on our own selfish desires, we have the wrong motives. I recommend that all intercessors, also the mature intercessors, often read James 4:2-3 and that we allow the Holy Spirit to be honest with us.

6. Idle words

God hates idle talk. The literal meaning of this phrase is to use words with no particular purpose or effect or to keep on repeating the same words; useless, meaningless words. So often our prayers just pay lip-service, the words are not from our hearts.

Think back to your prayers of the past week. What did you pray for this past week? Can you remember what you asked God? Will it make a difference in your life if God does not answer your prayers, or doesn't it really matter? When we have this attitude, our prayers will be an idle repetition of empty, meaningless words.

Someone once said, "God will never answer the casual enquirer."

7. A critical spirit

Many prayers come from critical hearts. Critical hearts are spiteful hearts that make accusations, pass judgment. The person with a critical heart cannot feel compassion and this means that this person cannot or will not bear another's burden. The true intercessor knows that everything the critical person says is most probably true and that much more could quite possibly be added. And that is exactly why he does not judge or accuse, but pleads with God for grace for the person he is interceding for. The true intercessor sees the sins and shortcomings of people and this makes him/her cry. The person with the critical spirit passes judgment and feels no compassion.

Obstacles to intercession

I would like to point out different things that could be obstacles in the life of the intercessor. Certain sins like bitterness and an unforgiving heart, a critical spirit, miserliness, a malfunctioning relationship between husband and wife, etcetera could be obstacles, but this is not something I want to discuss now.

1. Inadequate worship and praise

The first duty of a Christian is worship. This goes for an intercessor as well. As intercessors we cannot simply charge into God's presence and unpack our prayer requests before God. God wants a relationship with us. From this relationship with God, our intercession can ascend before the throne of God.

Worship and praise bring us into the correct relationship with God and it is from this relationship that we may call upon God's grace. Time spent on praise and worship could never ever be time wasted.

2. Praying from a position of fear

It often happens that we are driven to intercession by our fear. Fear destroys faith. God delights in those who come to Him and pray in faith and in the expectation that He will intervene in his omnipotence and turn around the situation.

Too often our intercession is motivated by fear and not by God's omnipotence.

3. Not praying in the Spirit

Twice we are encouraged to pray in the Spirit (Eph 6:18; Jude verse 20). I know that there is a difference of opinion about precisely what it means to pray in the Spirit. However, at the very least it means to pray under the guidance of the Holy Spirit. Only too often we work out our own prayers and present these to God and do not first seek the guidance of the Holy Spirit.

In conjunction with this concept is the whole aspect of listening. I had already written two books on prayer before the Lord taught me how to listen. Prayer is not a monologue. Prayer is a dialogue. Prayer is listening for the voice of God – praying under the guidance of the Holy Spirit. If we do not do this, our prayer becomes lame, impoverished and so much less effective. Then it is like firing a shot into the dark and calling out: May it hit something!

4. Whining

There are intercessors who are forever whining before God. There is a difference between petitioning, supplication and pleading with God, and complaining. Some intercessors constantly whine before God like children who wail and moan if they do not get their way. God wants people who pray to come to Him in brokenness of spirit and obedience to intercede for another. God is not impressed by our whining. There is nothing quite as irritating as someone who is always moaning and groaning. I know Christians who are permanent naggers – they nag God and everybody around them. Such prayers hinder God's work, because the basic motive of a nagger is not the will of God or the honour of God, but this person's own, selfish needs and wants. Many wives who pray for the salvation of their husbands are in fact more concerned about their own inconvenience and suffering when they pray that the honour of God be restored, their husbands will not perish and that Jesus will be exalted. Small wonder that these people pray for years and get no answers to their prayers.

5. Using methods and techniques to get answers to prayers

Intercession is not a method or technique. It is not the ability to use the correct expressions and specific prophetic action. Intercession is a relationship with God where the intercessor understands the heart of God and prays to a living God who is merciful and compassionate.

When I am asked to lead a prayer time, I seldom have an idea beforehand of how I will go about it. I simply arm myself with the thought that God is alive, that He promised the Holy Spirit as a Helper and that He will answer our prayers if we pray in the Name of Jesus Christ. There are no standard plans and techniques. Every prayer opportunity is unique. Intercession is a living, dynamic happening between God and a human and it cannot be captured in techniques and acquired methods. God is a God of relationships, not a God of techniques.

Wrong

ways to pray

Not this way

1. "Lord, break him"

Often in the past I sat in prayer meetings where people prayed, "Lord save/change that person, or break him/her." And the people who pray like this are good and solemn Christians. Christians often pray this in desperation. Church members sometimes pray this when their preacher does not walk with God, (in their opinion). Some women pray this for their unsaved husbands. We sometimes hear people pray: "Lord, save this person, change him, or kill him."

This type of prayer is wrong. I see nowhere in the Scriptures that God says we may pray that God breaks a person. Yes, the Bible teaches us about brokenness, but not that we must pray for someone to be broken by God. Neither does it say we can pray for ourselves, "Lord, break me". Or we don't like someone

and would prefer that this person disappears from our lives. In such situations we often find that people pray, for example, "Lord, that political leader's influence is doing a lot of harm to our country. Please relieve him of his position or break him (destroy him, etcetera)." Such prayers are unbiblical. Sometimes they also take on the form of a kind of curse that is pronounced on someone, something like the Old Testament Biblical curses.

Take note of Daniel's attitude when he interpreted King Nebuchadnezzar's dreams. He said, "My lord, if only the dream applied to your enemies and its meaning to your adversaries" (Dan 4:19)! Here was a godless king and yet Daniel did not have the attitude of: "Serves you right." Intercessors who have the Spirit of God in them will pray for God's grace and not for God's punishment.

It is true that God breaks people and brings brokenness, but then it is God's doing. God is God and He knows what to do and how to do it. I know of cases where Christians prayed, "Lord, break that person," and in the end that person was indeed broken. In some cases they became involved in unsavoury relationships, they became alcoholics or went through divorce. Often these people do not recover.

There are for example Christians who stand in front of pornographic book shops, night clubs, bars etcetera and pray that the places burn down. I am convinced these people are acting outside the will of God. Often one hears how Christians take passages from the psalms where David prayed that his enemies be consumed by worms or that they break their necks. I do not think that we as New Testament Christians have the right to pray these kinds of prayers. In Luke 9:54-56 the disciples ask Jesus if they should pray that God will destroy the Samaritans by fire as it happened during Elijah's lifetime, and Jesus rebuked them because of the attitude of their hearts.

This type of prayer is a poor testimony to unbelievers. What will unbelievers think when we pray, "Lord, save him/her or kill him"? What kind of gospel is this? Such prayers also violate the principle of God's grace. We read in John 1:16: *From the fullness of his grace we have all received one blessing after another.* In Habakkuk 3:2 we read that Habakkuk prays and asks God to please remember mercy in his wrath. Every intercessor should know that whatever he or she is, they are this only by virtue of God's grace. It is not our task to pray for the downfall of people or their destruction, but for their conversion and that Christ will take shape in them. It is not our task to judge either – judgment belongs to the Lord. Yes, we must distinguish between what is right and wrong, but the judgment is God's. Rebuke the Evil One that attacks people, controls and manipulates people – that is in line with the Scriptures. I am however convinced that we never, but never have the right to curse people, to condemn them or to pray for their destruction and downfall.

When we pray for difficult people or situations, our prayers should be in line with the spirit of the Bible:

- In the first place our prayers must be in line with God's law of love. Can I honestly say that when I pray for someone, "Lord, break him", that it is in line with the law of love?
- Secondly, our prayers should be according to the principle of God's grace and compassion. We can pray, "Lord, have mercy and bring this person to repentance and conversion." With this I can agree. If God chooses to answer my prayer by breaking the person, then that is all right, but then it is God working and answering in his sovereignty. In Luke 9:54-56 Jesus teaches us that the Son of Man did not come to destroy people's lives, but to save them. Our prayers must be in line with this.
- Many people refer to the psalms where David prayed that God would destroy his enemies. I hear what they say, but I am convinced that we should be exceptionally careful and stay within the guidelines of love, grace and compassion. I am not convinced that we can make David's prayers of

condemnation over his enemies applicable to our own situation just like that. So often the psalms teach us that God listens to the *righteous* and for them the promises are true. Let us live in righteousness and leave the judgment to God, as we are taught in Romans 12:19-21.

- What do we do when we receive a word of judgment from God? Pray for grace and ask God to be compassionate. In Habakkuk 3:2 the prophet Habakkuk prays, *"... in* [your] *wrath remember mercy."* When God pronounced his judgment over Israel after they worshipped the golden calf, Moses did not call out, "That's right, punish them". No, he pleaded with God to have mercy. Jeremiah is another example. He prayed to God for the recovery of the people of Israel. But at a certain point the Lord told Jeremiah to stop praying for the people (Jer 15:1). However, Jeremiah carried on pleading with the Lord and fifteen chapters later the Lord announced mercy.
- This type of "break him" prayer is not a good testimony to unbelievers. How will we convince unbelievers that God is a God of love if this is the way we pray for them?

2. "Lord, I command You ..."

I don't think we are on Scriptural ground when intercessors start giving God orders. Quite frankly, I think it is extremely arrogant. In many churches Christians are taught to demand certain things from God or to command God. I do not find evidence of this in the Bible.

There are those who think we can command God to give us a particular thing or to do something for us on the grounds of certain promises that God makes. Remember, however, that Satan came to tempt Jesus on the grounds of specific scriptures. Every time Jesus' answer was, *"Yes, but it is also written."* We must realise that we have a limited understanding of the Bible. Not all promises are valid at all times in all situations. We go through different growth processes, and circumstances differ and change. So we need to be careful.

I can strongly appeal to God for healing on the basis of Isaiah 53:4: *Surely he took up our infirmities and carried our sorrows.* But it will still happen that I die at some stage or another. As God heals sickness, it is also a law that we are all going to die. When Jesus commands his disciples to go out and heal people, it is clear from the Bible and in practice that not all are healed. All through history God used men and women to pray for the sick and thousands were healed. But it is also true that many were not healed – because God is still sovereign and He heals whom He wants to.

When we pray the promises of God, we should always do it with the following prayer in mind: "Father, your will be done." Why? Is it then not unbelief that makes us pray like this? No! We are human, we know in part and do not understand everything the way we should. We must come to God in faith, but we must also understand that we are imperfect in our understanding of certain situations and that is why we pray, "Lord, not my will, but your will be done."

3. Soul force prayers

I strongly recommend that that you read the book *Soul and Spirit,* by Jessie Penn-Lewis on this subject. Niel T. Anderson also explains the matter of spirit, soul and body in his book *Victory over the Darkness.*

Soul force prayer is a form of prayer that is normally very sincere, but very dangerous. Soul force prayers are from the soul and not from the spirit of a person. We humans consist of a spirit, soul and body. As believers we should pray from the spirit, under the guidance of the Holy Spirit. The soul of a human being is where the will, emotions, intellect and the self reside. Prayers from the soul are prayers where the person is guided by his emotions, will or intellect and in so doing, often disregards the guidance of the Holy Spirit. Soul force prayers are in a certain sense horizontal prayers; this is where the person who prays wants to change the situation with soul force. The consequence is that such a person does not seek and follow the guidance of the Holy Spirit and consequently starts to dictate to God what should happen; there is no mention of, "Lord, your will be done in this situation."

Such prayers often result in confusion, depression, spiritual "heaviness" or even sickness in the life of the person who is being prayed for. The word heaviness describes well the feeling a person gets when someone prays witchcraft prayers for (or rather against) him. In such circumstances where your state of mind is not caused by sickness or sin in your life, or is not the result of some or other disagreement present in your life, you can pray the following prayer: Father, in the Name of Jesus, I break every prayer that is prayed for me that is not in line with your will for my life. I resist and refuse the influence of manipulating and self-willed prayers.

We must pray for the will of God to be done. The self may never come in between. This is why it is so important to find out from God what we should pray for. Prayer from the spirit and in the Spirit is prayer that is inspired by the Holy Spirit, where the will, the emotions and the intellect of the person are subordinate to the will and guidance of God. Prayer from the spirit acknowledges the sovereignty of God, does not dictate to God, submits to the will of God and accepts God's answer.

Prayer from the spirit is prayer where we pray to the Father and leave our prayer with Him to solve in his own way.

In my own life I have often experienced the effect of soul force prayer. On occasion my wife and I made friends with someone who appeared to be a devoted Christian. In the course of time however we found out that she was part of a group with very extreme views. Without us knowing it, this group had started praying for us to go over to them and to accept their specific views. I was experiencing all the more "spiritual" pressure. It was literally like a heavy burden I was dragging along. One night I realised something was wrong and in the Name of Jesus I resisted this soul force prayer, asked the Lord to break the influence of these prayers by the power of the Holy Spirit and to just encourage me spiritually once more. At once it was as if someone physically lifted a heavy weight from my shoulders and spiritually there was also instant relief and more clarity on the road ahead.

In her book *Soul and Spirit,* Jessie Penn-Lewis writes about a minister who experienced extraordinary attacks from Evil and spiritual pressurisation. He became ill, his heart was affected, he haemorrhaged and he was short of breath. As time went by he became aware of five believers who were busy praying for him to "gain a different perspective". He realised that what these men had in mind was in direct conflict with the Word of God. He immediately called upon God and resisted the soul force prayers by which these men were forcing themselves on him. There was instant relief and gradually all the physical and spiritual symptoms disappeared with time.

4. Witchcraft prayers

The essence of witchcraft prayer is manipulation and this is born in someone who tries to get his own way and satisfy his own desires by means of supernatural powers. Witchcraft is artificial spiritual force and the abuse of supernatural powers for the person's own benefit. It is forcing people to do things that you want them to do. When we talk about witchcraft prayers, we mean prayers that are in their very essence selfish, manipulating, self-willed and centred on the self. Such prayers are not concerned with the will and honour of God. God does not allow people to use or abuse Him. God is not a lucky charm who must see to it that our wishes are granted and our desires satisfied. Many people use prayer in a way that has exactly the same character as magic. This type of prayer can also be described as prayer of the flesh. The self is at the centre and the will of God does not feature anywhere.

For example, a girl sees a man and falls in love with him at first sight. Now she starts asking the Lord for this man. Later she even gets the "scripture" that she is going to get married to this man and claims him from the Lord. Eventually they get married and the marriage doesn't work out. Where did things go wrong? At the point where the girl set her emotions and her love above the Lord's will. Her (selfish) desire was the reason why she missed out on the will of the Lord. This is what James 4:2-3 is talking about when he says that people pray with the wrong motives, because their prayer is all about their own pleasure and selfish needs.

This type of prayer places burdens, bondage and even curses on the person they are praying for. The fruit of this kind of prayer is negative in the long run. Such prayers release powerful psychic forces into the spiritual realm and restrict and harm the person they are praying for. These are once again prayers that are from the human being himself/herself and are focused on the needs of the self.

Cindy Jacobs writes in her book, *Possessing the Gates of the enemy,* (pp 136-139), how a friend phoned her on occasion and told her that the Lord had given her a word that she would get married to a certain evangelist whom she had not yet met. She asked, "Cindy, I want to ask you to pray with me and agree with me that I will meet this specific person and that we will get married afterwards." There were a few problems. Cindy had no conviction that the Lord wanted the two people to get married. Secondly God never spoke to the evangelist about this specific woman. The matter became more complicated when a second woman also phoned Cindy and told her that the Lord had very clearly confirmed with her that this same evangelist would get married to her. At least one of the two women, or both had misheard. God does not approve of polygamy. Her friend did not ask, "Won't you pray with me and ask what the Lord's will is?" Furthermore when it comes to the topic of marriage, the Lord must speak to both parties, not only to one person.

Cindy went on and prayed that the Lord would send the right person into her friend's life as a marriage partner, that the person would be a Christian, and that she would only pray with her if the Lord confirmed directly with her that He indeed wanted both people to be joined together in holy matrimony.

Here we have a clear-cut case of witchcraft prayer. It was a woman who fell in love with a person, had a strong desire to get married to this person and started looking for confirmation of her emotions in the Bible. Furthermore she started manipulating God through prayer to grant her wish.

We often find this type of prayer with domineering persons, people who are strongly manipulative, and in cases where people have such a desire or need for something that they cannot come and stand objectively and neutrally before God to seek his will.

This type of prayer is found in many situations:

- someone who wants a specific house or property;
- someone who has a strong obsession to be rich and have many possessions;
- someone who desires a specific position;
- someone who wants to be acknowledged or wants to realise an own dream or pursue an ambition.

These situations and many more, could open the door to prayers that are not in line with the Bible. Witchcraft prayers can release psychic energy that is very negative and could throw open the doors to demonic forces. The words that we speak have a powerful effect. Proverbs 18:21 says, *"The tongue has the power of life and death ..."* Demons can establish a stronghold by means of such prayers because the self and not the will of God is at the centre.

5. "I take his/her sin/sickness/weakness on me"

Another extremely dangerous form of prayer is when people start praying with great empathy for others: "Lord, I take this person's sin/sickness/ weakness on me. I am willing to bear it." This type of prayer opens the door to the devil to bring sickness upon us. Although the prayer is directed at God, it is not Scriptural. That is why the devil can bring disease in such a case and if we do not resist it, it could destroy and impede our lives.

In the USA there was a case of an intercessor who fell ill. (This information is taken from a book by Dr Andrew Murray). This woman had prayed and said to the Lord that she was prepared to take the illness of another person that she knew on her. She did not believe it could really make her sick. She believed it was merely the symptoms of the illness that she was busy suffering from. The intercessor became sicker by the day and eventually she saw a doctor where it was determined that she was suffering from diabetes, which was already at an advanced stage. Her condition deteriorated and eventually she died. This is a case of somebody praying incorrectly with good intentions and the consequences were destructive.

The Scriptures are quite clear about the fact that Jesus took our sins and sickness on Him. It is not necessary that we try to bear another's sin or sickness. In any event, we can't. Was what Jesus did insufficient? Of course we will all answer "no". Why then would we want to take the sickness, weakness or sin of others on us?

The lives of many Christians have been destroyed because they prayed this type of prayer. It is not for us to take the sickness, weakness or sins of others on us, but to take it to the Father and to plead with the Father on the grounds of the perfected work of Jesus on the cross. We bring the sickness, sins and weaknesses of others to the Father on the grounds that Jesus has already taken these on Him. We cannot add anything to that.

The concept *identification* is used in many circles and there is room for it in intercession. When the concept *identification,* however, takes on the meaning that I take another's sins, sickness and weakness on me and try to bear it, then we have taken it too far.

Although I have great respect for the ministry of Rees Howells and learnt a lot from his biography, *Intercessor,* I am convinced that the manner in which his biographer, Norman Grubb describes how Rees Howells prayed for the sick, opens the door to misunderstanding. He describes how Rees Howells literally took the illness of the sick on himself when praying for their healing. I am not convinced that we have Scriptural testimony to venture onto this level. Jesus Christ has already taken the sickness, weakness and sins of all of humanity on Him. It is not our task to do it all over again. Our identification consists of empathy with that person and to take his/her ailment, sin or weakness to the throne of grace, and on the grounds of Jesus' perfected work on the cross, approach the throne of grace in great confidence. 1 Peter 2:24 teaches us: *He himself bore our sins in his body on the tree, so that we may die to sins and live for righteousness; by his wounds you have been healed.*

It can happen that when you intercede for someone as intercessor, you suddenly experience the same symptoms or the same temptations as that person you are praying for. Many intercessors then think that in this way they are bearing that person's burden. We should however remember that when we intercede for someone, Satan will attack us and often he attacks us on the same territory as the person we are busy praying for. We must not allow this to confuse us. In such situations these temptations or sickness or symptoms must be radically and directly withstood. If Satan does not succeed in harming the particular person you are praying for, he would not mind turning to the intercessor. Let us be watchful and vigilant.

Safety mechanisms

How can we guard against these pitfalls? The following are a few principles that you can apply in your prayer life:

- Your prayers should be a blessing to others. Ask yourself repeatedly if your prayers are in line with the principle of God's grace and the law of love for your neighbour.
- You must receive your prayer burdens from God through the Holy Spirit.
- Your life must be clean and free of any form of conscious, unconfessed sin.
- The self must be crucified.
- Nourish yourself daily with the Word of God.
- Do not follow new forms of prayer just like that. Put them to the test by using the Bible. Make sure there are really Scriptural grounds for the way in which you pray.
- With your will, choose in any situation to seek God's will and do it and pray it.
- You must examine yourself regularly for any form of haughtiness, manipulation, bitterness or jealousy.
- Learn to pray the Scriptures. Examine the Scriptures and see how the intercessors in the Bible prayed. Look especially at the prayers of Paul. Don't just take scriptures left and right and pray them. Sometimes we pray that the Lord will take away sickness or financial pressure from a person while it is often actually the very things the Lord wants to use to teach the person more obedience, faith and dependency. Get your scriptures from God before you pray them.
- Make sure your prayers are in line with the principles of love, grace and compassion.

21

Intercessors must have clean hands

Lifting up holy hands

A few years back it was unheard of for people to physically lift up their hands to God. This even gave rise to theological dispute. Today it is accepted more readily. We find at least 37 references in the Old and New Testament that believers should and may lift up their hands to God. But this is also qualified: we must lift up holy hands.

We read in 1 Timothy 2:8 that Paul encourages believers with a clear conscience, to lift up holy hands to God in prayer, wherever they gather together. Psalm 24:3-4 asks a question and answers it: *Who may ascend the hill of the Lord? Who may stand in his holy place? He who has clean hands and a pure heart ...*Those who stand in God's presence, must have clean hands. How much more should this apply to intercessors? Would God hear an intercessor who stands before Him with unclean hands? In Matthew 5:8 Jesus promises: *Blessed are the pure in heart, for they will see God.* What a great promise, but how unmistakable the condition!

Recently I discovered a precious promise in Job 22:29-30: *"When men are brought low and you say, 'Lift them up!' then he will save the downcast. He will deliver even one who is not innocent, who will be delivered through the cleanness of your hands."* A paraphrase would be: The Lord will save the guilty and restore them through the cleanness of the intercessor's hands. Intercessors must lift up holy hands to God and then He will save the godless and the sinner.

It is so easy to say to someone, "Just pray, the Lord will give you what you ask for," or "Pray for your husband/wife/child/friend. God will surely save him/her." Yes, that is true, but the requirement of the Bible is that we pray with clean hands. The same thought is also found in Psalm 66:18: *"If I had cherished sin in my heart, the Lord would not have listened."* In Proverbs 28:9 and 13 we find these words: *"If anyone turns a deaf ear to the law, even his prayers are detestable ... He who conceals his sins does not prosper, but whoever confesses and renounces them finds mercy."*

We must be under no illusions: God never ever compromises with sin. You might have experienced a thousand answers to prayer, seen tens of thousands of miracles in answer to prayer, but if you allow sin in your life, God will not answer you. Isaiah 59:1-2 is quite clear: *"Surely the arm of the Lord is not too short to save, nor his ear too dull to hear. But your iniquities have separated you from your God; your sins have hidden his face from you, so that he will not hear."*

Unclean hands and spiritual warfare

One night I was busy praying with someone. For close on two

hours we were engaged in intensive prayer warfare. Yet there was no breakthrough. It was getting late and we were physically tired and also despondent. At about half past eleven I said to my friend, "It is as if I can see the finish line, as if I am already experiencing the victory, but something is holding us back. What is it?" We stopped praying and lay prostrate before the Lord. The Holy Spirit distinctly pointed out to me some anger in my heart. Something had happened a few days before and there was anger in my heart. I confessed it before the Lord. The next moment the breakthrough was there. Without further prayer, without dramatic faith or struggle, the victory was there and we could go to bed. That night the Lord showed me that one "tiny piece" of anger in my heart made room for the devil and was the cause that we could not gain the victory in this particular battle.

On another occasion a friend and I were busy praying for someone who was possessed by demons. By half past twelve the demons would not let go their hold over the person. We prayed, pleaded with God to reveal his power and we proclaimed the promises of victory. We sang all the songs we knew that dealt with the blood of the Lamb. Nothing happened. We were exhausted and at our wits' end. In desperation we asked the Lord, "What is preventing the victory and the breakthrough?" After we had become still before the Lord, two "tiny" things came up in my heart that I knew grieved the Lord. I confessed them. My friend also confessed one or two things. Then we waited quietly on the Lord. The next moment God came through the power of the Holy Spirit and drove out those demons. Again it had been our sin that stood in the way of victory.

So often I find Christians who are seriously busy with spiritual and prayer warfare. They use all kinds of techniques and methods and the right words. People literally sweat it out as they pray, but the result is insignificant. I want to simply ask,

"What do your hands look like?" Getting involved in prayer warfare without my life being clean before God, is the ultimate in foolishness.

Many Christians "plead the blood" over them when they are involved in spiritual warfare. Yes, our victory is in the blood of the Lamb. But the blood of Jesus will "cover" nothing that has not been confessed first. Duncan Campbell, God's instrument in the Hebridean revival, said, "Calvary will never cover what we have to uncover." The blood does not conceal the sin, the blood cleanses from sin – and we are only cleansed of our sin when we confess it before God and renounce it.

Walk in the light

We must walk in the light every day. This means to stand in God's light daily so that our whole life is illuminated. Nothing must be in the darkness. When we stand in God's light, in his presence, his light shines on us and our sin, and impurities become clear to us. Then we know what we should confess before God.

The message of 1 John 3:21-22 is clear: *... if our hearts do not condemn us, we have confidence before God and receive from him anything we ask, because we obey his commands and do what pleases him.* Here are three explicit conditions for answers to prayer: if our conscience does not condemn us, in other words, if our lives are clean before God and the Spirit of God does not point out to us any sin or impurity; if we obey God's commandments; if we do what pleases Him. God works according to certain spiritual laws that He made Himself. One of these laws is that we must approach Him with a clear conscience, a conscience that does not condemn us.

More than plans and methods

E.M. Bounds was one of those men who practised what he preached. He wrote many books on prayer and he was a man who prayed. Bounds made much of the person who prays, of the intercessor. Plans and methods were subordinate to the person who prays and to prayer.

In his book, *The Power of Prayer,* he writes: "We are constantly busy contemplating new methods, new plans and new organisations to let the church grow and to acquire expansion and effectiveness for the gospel. This tendency of our time is busy losing sight of the man and he is being absorbed by the plan or organisation. God's plan is to make much of the man, much more of him than anything else. Man is God's method. The church looks for better methods; God looks for better men ... What the church needs today, is not more machines or better machinery, not better organisations or more and newer methods, but men who can be used by the Holy Spirit – men of prayer, men who are mighty in prayer. The Holy Spirit does not flow through methods, but through men. He does not come for machines, but for men. He does not anoint plans, but men – men of prayer."

22

The discipline and price of intercession

Intercession requires discipline. It asks me to be available for the Spirit and to obey Him absolutely, unrelentingly and immediately. Intercessors are people who must live *under the discipline of the Holy Spirit*, otherwise they will not be able to gain the victory in and through intercession. The discipline of the Holy Spirit asks that I as intercessor must be instantly available when the Holy Spirit calls on me to intercede for someone or a matter. An intercessor who talks back, argues, first wants to rest a while or first wants to do something else, will grieve the Holy Spirit. When we resist the Spirit like this, we will eventually quench Him and He will not make any further use of us in intercession.

Intercession is a position before God. It is a spiritual position before God, a 24-hour position. This position requires perseverance – to carry on praying until the prayer burden disappears, until the answer comes, until the Holy Spirit sets us free to carry on with other tasks. It requires sacrifice. It wants a sacrifice that I do not benefit from in any way. Others benefit. We are so used to it that we must be rewarded or blessed in some way. The whole world, the advertising world, the business world, everybody tries to teach us that our own interests are number one. In intercession, the exact opposite is true. The intercessor says no to his/her own needs, yes to the needs of others.

It asks that I will set aside myself, my needs, my desires (food, sleep, comfort) and pray until God answers. I must remain in that position because God has called me to do it. If I do not obey, it can be of great harm to the kingdom of God or to the individual/group/cause that I am praying for. Intercession asks for time, a lot of time – it wants me to give "my" time for the salvation or recovery of someone else. Intercession wants my emotions, it wants my tears, it asks me to cry with those who cry and that I have compassion with those in need. Are you able to cry about another's sin? Can you put yourself in the place of that one ungodly, God-less, despicable sinner and pray for him/her as if you yourself or your closest and best friend is in that state?

What an example of an intercessor we have in the Lord Jesus! We read in Hebrews 5:7 that He "offered up prayers and petitions with loud cries and tears" to God, his Father, and that He was heard. Jesus cried about us. He could cry about Jerusalem that had strayed and He cried because Lazarus had died. Intercession asks for our emotions and our tears. In Gethsemane Jesus' intercession caused Him such agony that He had difficulty breathing and felt as if He was dying – because of the burden of our sins on Him. There in Gethsemane He wrestled with God for our sins until his sweat was like drops of blood falling to the ground. In Gethsemane Jesus wrestled with the Father and it cost Him his life. Because Jesus was willing to intercede for the world, it cost Him his life.

Intercession never comes cheap. Intercession involves my

entire being. It asks my everything. It was true in Jesus' life and it was true of many other intercessors. It might be that God could ask the same of you. The question is quite simple: Are you prepared to pay the price of intercession? We would like to be known as intercessors and we like talking about how God answered *our* prayers (and we tend to forget that it was *God* who answered them), but we are so seldom willing to pay the price. And this is why people sometimes pray and do not get answers to their prayers.

Intercession wants me to identify with the person (his situation, sin, etc). I must put myself in the person's place. I must take his place before the throne of God and plead with God for him/her. And when I pray, it often happens that I have to pray for a brother or a sister who has sinned. Sometimes it is a murderer, at other times a rapist or a thief or someone who wronged me. There was a day that Abraham had to pray for Abimelech because Abimelech wanted to take Abraham's wife Sarah as wife. Abraham acted as intercessor so that Abimelech could be saved – the man who wanted his wife. Job had to pray for his three friends, act as intercessor, before God forgave them and restored them. These were the three friends who made life so difficult for Job with their arguments and accusations, and yet God chose *Job* to pray for them.

In God's presence

Why are so few people intercessors? There are many people who pray, but few intercessors. An intercessor is someone who has to spend time in God's presence, a lot of time. Few people feel up to it. An intercessor is someone who dares to enter into the presence of the living God and to talk to God. Yes, it is true that God is love, that He is a merciful God, that He is compassionate and good. Many Bible figures found God's presence an unnerving experience. Take Moses at the burning bush, Jacob at Bethel, the prophet Isaiah who saw God in a vision in the temple (Isa 6), Elijah in the cave at Mount Horeb, John on the island of Patmos.

We read in Hebrews 12:29, *"... our God is a consuming fire."* Daniel 7:9-10 teaches us that God's throne is "flaming with fire" and that a river of fire flows from the throne. Whoever wishes to come near the "throne" of God must pass through that blazing fire to God. The fire is there to consume all that is impure and unclean so that nothing impure can come near the throne. Only those who bear the stamp of humbleness and live a pure and holy life will survive in the presence of God.

We read about Daniel, the beloved man of God, that when the angel of God came to him, he fell prostrate to the ground as a result of the splendour of the angel. The apostle John had the same experience in the book of Revelation. This is what happens when angels appear to people. What will happen when we enter into the presence of God? Think about it that Daniel is the only person who is called "a beloved man of God", and that it is written in Daniel 6 that they could find no corruption in Daniel, that he did nothing wrong, nothing big or small.

Jacob was in God's presence in a dream, not even in full reality. In Genesis 28:16-17 we read, *"Surely the Lord is in this place, and I was not aware of it." He* [Jacob] *was afraid and said, "How awesome is this place!"* Jacob was afraid. Why did he find the place awesome? Because of the presence of God!

Intercessors are people who must be in the presence of God daily. In this presence there is no room for the self, sin, pride, licentiousness, impurity, lust, frivolity and wilfulness. Are we not told in the Scriptures that no one can see God and stay alive? This is the truth, spiritually: those who want to see God must die to self, they must "die", otherwise they will not be able to see God. And this is where the problem lies: our sin and our love of sin and the world make God's presence unbearable even to many Christians. We want God's blessings, protection, gifts and salvation, but we are uncomfortable in his presence.

Dying to self

In his lifetime, George Mueller wrote down 50 000 direct answers to prayer. He never made his needs known to people. His aim was to illustrate to the church of his day that God answers fervent, prevailing and faithful prayer. He built numerous orphanages and cared for more than 4 000 children daily – by means of prayer. On occasion someone came to him and asked him what his secret was. Why was it that he saw so many of his prayers answered? Bending down lower and lower, until he almost touched the ground, he said that there had been a day that he died, died completely, died to George Mueller, his opinions, his own way of understanding things, taste and will, died to the approval and disapproval of his brothers and friends, and ever since, he had merely endeavoured to present himself pleasing in the sight of God.

D.L. Moody was one of the greatest evangelists of the previous century. A young man asked him one day, "Mr Moody, what does it mean to die to yourself?" Moody got up and asked the young man to follow him. He walked to the cemetery, stood at a graveside and said to the young man, "Insult the man lying here, malign him." The young man protested. Eventually Moody got the young man to mumble a few negative words. Then Moody told the young man to praise the man buried there, to flatter him and pay him compliments. Once again a few uninspired words came from the lips of the flabbergasted and astonished young man. Then Moody asked him, "What did the man do when you insulted him?" The young man answered, "Nothing, he is dead." Again Moody asked a question, "And what did he do when you praised him?" Again the answer:

"Nothing. The man is dead. He cannot react." To this Moody replied, "This is what it means to die to yourself. You are dead to the world, the approval and disapproval of people, their insults and their praise. Someone who has died does not react to any influence of the world."

Would you still be prepared?

The characteristics of an Intercessor

1. An intercessor must persevere

The Bible teaches us to persist in prayer. In a previous chapter I wrote about *travail.* Here however, I want to draw your attention to the fact that perseverance is part of the character of the intercessor.

Daniel prayed, ate dry bread and drank only water for 21 days, waiting for the answer to come. Elijah sent his servant back seven times to go and see if there was any sign of rain. Moses lay prostrate before God on the mountain for 40 days without food and water and pleaded that God would not destroy Israel. Jacob wrestled with the angel until daybreak, but he did not give up. Because they persevered, God answered.

Jesus says in Luke 18 that we must keep on praying. It is a command. Yet so few Christians manage to persevere.

A female mouse gives birth to baby mice seven days after conception. An elephant cow is in calf for 22 months. But what a difference in the product delivered! You can pick a corn-cob less than six months after you planted the seed. To grow a full-sized Oak tree takes a hundred years or more. But what a difference between a corn-cob and an oak tree!

The difference lies in time, perseverance, persistence.

2. Intercessors see the unseen

To believe, says Hebrews 11:1 *... is being sure of what we hope for and certain of what we don't see.* To me, this is a description of an intercessor. Intercessors are people who see "visions". They "see" things in the spirit and then pray about these until they become reality. Intercessors believe in God, their hope is in God. They pray like people who see the unseen as if it already exists. Because they see it with their spiritual eyes, they pray and persist in prayer until God brings it about.

3. Intercessors are willing to lay down their lives

Intercessors have the same approach that Jesus had. Jesus laid down his life for the sins of the world. There is clear evidence of this approach in the lives of Paul and Moses.

In Exodus 32:32 Moses says, *"But now, please forgive their* [Israel's] *sin – but if not, then blot me out of the book you have written."* Moses is so serious when he prays that God will forgive Israel that he is prepared to give his life so that Israel can be saved.

In Romans 9:3 Paul says, *"For I could wish that I myself were cursed and cut off from Christ for the sake of my brothers ..."* Here we find precisely the same attitude as that of Moses. Paul is prepared to be cursed by God, cut off from life, if it could contribute to the salvation of the Jews.

In Genesis 18 we read that Abraham was prepared to put his life at stake by praying for Sodom and Gomorrah. We read in

Genesis 18:27 that Abraham says, *"Now that I have been so bold as to speak to the Lord, though I am nothing but dust and ashes …"*

It is important to note that God does not ask us to take the curse of another's sin on us – Jesus Christ has already done that. I however, believe that every true intercessor has the same attitude as Christ, namely to be willing to lay down our lives for others.

Can we cry about the sins of others, the unsaved, or are we so caught up in the rush of providing for our own needs and seeing to our own comforts, that we couldn't really care less what happens to others?

Someone who does not love and who cannot cry cannot be an intercessor. The attitude of the intercessor is defined in the words of Romans 5:8: *… God demonstrates his own love for us in this: While we were still sinners, Christ died for us.*

Do we have this attitude?

4. Intercessors are passionate about souls

John 3:16 reveals to us the heart of God: *"For God so loved the world that he gave his one and only Son, that whoever believes in him shall not perish but have eternal life."* God is passionate about souls – he does not want people to perish, He wants people to be saved. Jesus' act of intercession on the cross was for the sake of the salvation of people.

There are examples in history of intercessors who revealed this character. One of them was John Hyde from India. He was known as "Praying Hyde". He laid down his life for the people of the Punjab. John Hyde literally prayed himself to death. At the end of his life doctors found that his heart was enlarged and had moved to the right-hand side of his chest. According to them this man must have experienced exceptional heartache and trauma. He had. Day and night he was busy pleading before God as intercessor for the salvation of Indians. John Hyde died at the age of 47. When I read his biography, *The Praying Hyde,* I realised that I still understood so little about intercession.

At the beginning of 1908 John Hyde reached the stage where he trusted God for the salvation of one person a day. By the end of that year there were 400 baptised converts who were built into the church of Christ as living stones. The following year, 1909, he wrestled with God until he had the faith for the salvation of two people a day – 800 came in. By 1910 the Lord augmented John Hyde's faith and he trusted God for four souls a day. Every day John Hyde led at least four people to the Lord. These people were not only converts; they became disciples.

In Matthew 9:36 we read that Jesus had compassion with the people, He felt deeply sorry for them. And it was because of this compassion that He called on his disciples to pray to God for workers for the harvest field. Without compassion we could never be true intercessors. The word compassion is a compound of two Latin words *cum* and *pati*. The word *cum* means "together with" and the word *pati* means "to suffer" or "to be hurt". This brings out the meaning of the word compassion very well: to hurt or suffer with someone. Compassion is at the heart of intercession. It is more than feeling sorry for someone. It is dynamic love, active love. Jesus did not only pray for humanity, He suffered for us, became involved in our need and pain. It was his compassion that led to the act of intercession on the cross.

5. Intercessors have respect and regard for God

Intercessors understand that intimacy with God is not the same as familiarity. People often confuse these two concepts.

The intercessor associates with God on a very intimate level. Every day, for hours at a time he/she spends time in God's presence. Intercessors get to know God at a deeper level.

Too often intercessors go too far and they become familiar with God. God allows us in his presence, but He does not raise us to his level. We do not become equal to God. When intercessors cross this boundary, pride enters their hearts. Many think they are so special that they are on the same level as God and they become presumptuous. It is then that people start taking liberties and "command" God to do certain things, that they begin making demands and get to a point that they think they have some kind of hold over God.

The apostle John wrote five of the books of the New Testament. He was one of the three who knew Jesus best and is known in the Bible as "the disciple whom Jesus loved". He was the one who leaned back against Jesus' chest during the Last Supper. He was the apostle of love. During the time that he was in exile on the island of Patmos, he was busy worshipping God one Sunday morning. It is described in Revelation 1:9-17. Suddenly he heard a voice *behind* him. John was busy worshipping God but God was not where he thought he was; God was *behind* him. John was the one person on earth who most probably knew Jesus best. And yet, on that Sunday morning, when He saw the transfigured Jesus, he described Jesus as "someone like the Son of man". He did not turn around, see Jesus walking among the lamp stands, recognise Him and call out, "Hello, Jesus." It was the transfigured Jesus, the One whose feet were like bronze glowing in a furnace, and whose voice was like the sound of rushing waters. In his right hand he held seven stars, and a sharp double-edged sword came out of his mouth. His whole appearance was like the sun shining in all its brilliance.

When John saw the transfigured Jesus he fell at his feet like a dead person. If this was the effect the transfigured Jesus had on the apostle John, where do we stand? Let us understand who God is, who Jesus is and who the Holy Spirit is, and let our attitude towards God be one of reverence.

6. Intercessors are fighters

Intercessors are fighters. Intercession is at its very essence, wrestling. Intercession is wrestling with God and a battle against the forces of Evil. Many people cannot do the work of intercession, because they don't have fighting spirit.

Intercessors *wrestle in the first place, with God.* Jesus wrestled with his Father in Gethsemane. In Matthew 4 we read how Satan came to tempt Jesus and how Jesus was in a struggle with Evil. Jacob wrestled with the Angel until daybreak. But he did not let go of the Angel before He blessed him. Paul was engrossed in travailing prayer and prayed day and night, until Christ took shape in the Galatians. Abraham wrestled with God for Sodom and Gomorrah. Moses wrestled with God on the mountain and pleaded for the preservation of Israel.

In Luke 11:5-11 Jesus teaches his disciples to pray and He tells them the story of the unashamed friend. This "friend" is a reference to God. The man who had the visitors "wrestled" with his friend (God) for three loaves. In Luke 18:1-8 we have a reference to the widow and the difficult judge – the widow "defeats" the heartless judge. This is a lesson in perseverance, to struggle in prayer until you have got what you asked for.

Intercessors *wrestle in the second place against the forces of darkness.* Ephesians 6:12 warns us that our struggle is not against flesh and blood, but against the forces of evil in the heavens.

Intercessors inevitably come up against the forces of darkness. I have experienced it over and over again. When God reveals certain things to the intercessor and he/she starts praying for these, Satan and his demonic forces will try to be a hindrance. A battle is the inevitable result.

7. An intercessor is someone who trusts God

Some years ago my father and I sat in church one evening. He was a farmer in the Kalahari in Namibia. It had been a good rain season and he knew that the dry winter season would arrive within three months. From April to July grass fire hazard in the Kalahari is usually at its highest. Particularly during April and

May when there are late rains and the lightning strikes, the dry grass is easily set alight and a fire starts.

While he was sitting in church, my father decided that he would go to town the following day to take out insurance on the fields. Suddenly an idea struck him, "Why don't you insure your fields with Me?" After careful consideration he was convinced that the suggestion had come from the Lord. He decided not to insure his fields with the usual companies that year, but with God. The money for the monthly premiums he gave as a thanks-offering to different people as the Lord directed him.

One evening in May there was thunder and a strong wind. It was typical weather for grass fires. At about ten o'clock that night my father's neighbour phoned to say his grass fields were on fire. My father saw the red glow through the window. The lightning had set fire to the fields and a strong wind was blowing. If my father called farmers in the vicinity to come and help him it would take a few hours before they could do something about the fire and the damage would already have been done. He fell down onto his knees and cried out to God, "Lord, I am helpless, just You can stop the fire. I trust You." When he had prayed, he got up and looked out of the window. The red glow was not so bright anymore and gradually it disappeared completely.

The following morning he drove out into the fields, but he could find no sign of the grass fire. Somewhere a miracle had taken place. A few weeks later there was a strong wind again one afternoon and the typical thunderstorm that caused grass fires. Some days later my father came upon a black spot in the grass fields where the lightning has set fire to it that afternoon, but a rain shower came down on the spot and doused the flames. The first time my father had seen the fire and God intervened. The second time he had not seen the grass fire but God who sees everything, intervened once again and sent rain. In both cases God protected the grass fields that were insured with Him.

Intercessors are people who trust in God. They are people who throw themselves on God and cling firmly to what He told them. They know that God is not a liar, that God is not a human being, that God does not say something and then not do it (Num 23:19). Intercessors know they can trust God, because *they know God's character.* Abraham went to Mount Moriah to sacrifice his son, Isaac. He trusted God. God honoured Abraham because Abraham honoured God by obeying Him.

We read in Hebrews 11:6 *... anyone who comes to him* [God] *must believe that he exists and that he rewards those who earnestly seek him.* In John 14:1 Jesus teaches us: *"Do not let your hearts be troubled. Trust in God; trust also in me."*

8. Intercessors are not full of themselves

The watermark of an intercessor is brokenness. Intercessors cannot afford pride, because God resists the proud and gives grace to the humble. Intercessors live a very special life in God's presence every day, and in the presence of God nobody can afford to be full of themselves.

A scripture which is becoming more and more precious to me is Philippians 2:5-11. Jesus, the Son of God drained Himself or emptied Himself and took on the nature of a servant. One translation says, *"He emptied Himself and He took the nature of a servant."* The NIV says, *"He became nothing."* The Amplified Bible translates as follows: *"He stripped Himself of all privileges and rightful dignity so as to assume the guise of a servant (slave)."*

To act as intercessor Jesus had to empty Himself, become nothing, take on the nature of a slave or a servant. Only when He had done that, He was ready to do the work of intercessor. As intercessor He had no rights. A slave has no rights and privileges, ambitions and dreams. A slave does not have his own plans, but just carries out orders. The watermark of a good slave is obedience. Jesus was obedient, yes until death. It is because of his obedience that God gave Him a position above all authority, might and power and sovereignty and above every name. God raised Him above all things and before Him every knee will bend. But first He had to empty himself, become nothing, take on the nature of a slave. What immense spiritual depth is found in these few verses.

Intercessors are servants, not masters who rule over others. That is why intercessors can handle authority. They know that absolute obedience is imperative to the life of intercession and that is why they submit themselves to the will of God, the authority of the Word and the guidance of the Holy Spirit. The intercessor's only desire is to please the Father.

Jesus says in John 5:19 that He does nothing on his own, by Himself. He does only what He sees the father do. In John 5:30 He says, *"By myself I can do nothing."* In John 6:38 and 4:34 Jesus says quite clearly that He came to do the will of his Father. In John 7:16 He goes on to say that what He teaches the people is not his own teaching, but it comes from the Father. He teaches the people what the Father told Him to. In John 8:42 Jesus also says that He did not come to earth out of his own, but that He came because the Father sent him. What a perfect example Jesus set of the concept "to take on the nature of a servant".

9. Intercessors must have the attitude of Christ

In Psalm 106:23 we read about Moses who took the position of an intercessor before God. We read: *So he said he would destroy them – had not Moses, his chosen one, stood in the breach before him to keep his wrath from destroying them.* We read a more comprehensive story of Moses' intercession in Exodus 32 and Deuteronomy 9. We read how Moses, after 40 days of fasting, going without food and water, came back from the mountain where he was in the presence of God. When Moses came back to the camp, the Israelites were busy worshipping a golden calf. The Lord was infuriated. He was angry with the people of Israel and wanted to destroy them. He told Moses that He would take him (Moses) and make him into a mighty nation and destroy Israel. Moses however, shows that he is a true leader and an intercessor. His reaction is different to what ours would most probably have been. We would most likely have said, "Yes, Lord, the people have sinned terribly, they should be punished … and, Lord it is a good decision that you made to choose me to become a great nation. You will not regret it Lord that you chose me." But Moses replies, "No, Lord, rather blot my name out of your book, but spare the people of Israel."

During the first 40-day fast the Lord revealed many things to Moses on the mountain. These revelations are recorded in Exodus 19:31. The second time Moses went up the mountain, he stayed without food and water for 40 days again, but this time it was to stand in the breach for the people. He wrestled with God and pleaded that God would spare the people. This was a fast of humiliation. We read in Deuteronomy 9:25: *"I lay prostrate before the Lord those forty days and forty nights because the Lord had said he would destroy you.*"

Moses said in Exodus 32:32, *"But now please forgive their sin – but if not, then blot me out of the book you have written."* Here we have an attitude that should be the attitude of every intercessor. Moses is saying here that he would rather perish as long as the people of Israel are saved. We find the same attitude in Paul in Romans 9:3: *For I could wish that I myself were cursed and cut off from Christ for the sake of my brothers …*

It is this attitude of Moses that, I believe, tipped the scale. Jesus also had this same attitude. It did not cost Moses his life, but it cost Jesus his. Jesus laid down his life for the world and in so doing, opened the door for sinners to be saved. In anticipation of Jesus, the Messiah who would come, Moses prayed with the attitude of the Messiah and he is heard by virtue of the price that Jesus would pay almost 2000 years later for Israel and the sins of the world.

Intercessors who have the attitude of Jesus, will be powerful intercessors, they will achieve much. Of course God would not accept the offer of Moses and Paul or from anyone to die for someone else's sins, because Jesus has already paid that price; it does not have to be paid again. Moses succeeded because he had the attitude of Christ. Anyone who has the attitude of Christ, in this case the willingness to lay down his/her life for another, will have power with God.